# It's Complicated
## How Out Nation Is Coming Together and Falling Apart

# It's Complicated
## How Out Nation Is Coming Together and Falling Apart

Salena Zito

Creators Publishing
Hermosa Beach, CA

*IT'S COMPLICATED*
*How Our Nation Is Coming Together and Falling Apart*
Copyright © 2020 CREATORS PUBLISHING

*All rights reserved. No part of this book may be reproduced or transmitted in any form or by any means, electronic or mechanical, including photocopying, recording or by any information storage and retrieval system, without permission in writing from the author.*

**Cover art by Pete Kaminski**

**CREATORS PUBLISHING**
737 3rd St
Hermosa Beach, CA 90254
310-337-7003

*Although the author and publisher have made every effort to ensure that the information in this book was correct at press time, the author and publisher do not assume and hereby disclaim any liability to any party for any loss, damage or disruption caused by errors or omissions, whether such errors or omissions result from negligence, accident or any other cause.*

ISBN (print): 978-1-949673-36-4
ISBN (ebook): 978-1-949673-35-7

**First Edition**
Printed in the United States of America
1  3  5  7  9  10  8  6  4  2

# A Note From the Publisher

Since 1987, Creators has syndicated many of your favorite columns to newspapers. In this digital age, we are bringing collections of those columns to your fingertips. This will allow you to read and reread your favorite columnists, with your own personal digital archive of their work.
—Creators Publishing

# Contents

| | |
|---|---|
| American Civic Life tries to Make a Comeback | 1 |
| From Tea Party Insurgent to Last Man Standing: Ron Johnson in Wisconsin | 5 |
| Rick Scott Chased the Hispanic Vote and Got It | 8 |
| Amtrak Forgot Trains Aren't Planes | 11 |
| Nostalgia and the American Dream Aren't Airy Fantasies | 14 |
| Howard Schultz Unifies the Parties–Against Him | 17 |
| A Surprise Virtual Visit From the President | 20 |
| The Populist Sledgehammer Kills Amazon Jobs that Middle American Would Love to Have | 24 |
| While National Media Carried Water for Jussie Smollett, Local Media Did It Right | 28 |
| Trump's Anti-Socialist Strength Could Turn Venezuelan-Americans Into Republicans for Decades | 31 |
| Losing a Hometown Hero | 34 |
| From the Rubble of a Church Rises a Spirit of Love | 37 |
| Beto O'Rourke: Late-term Abortions Are 'About Women Making Their Own Decisions About Their Own Body' | 40 |
| Blue-Collar Worker Bashed by Trump, Wooed by Beto O'Rourke in Saem Week | 43 |
| How Pete Buttigieg Could Hurt Trump in the Rust Belt | 46 |
| An Answer to the Cost of College and Community Collapse: Community Colleges | 50 |
| After Mueller, Nobody Has Changes Their Views on Trump | 53 |
| Why Trump Is Bitter the Firefighters Endorsed Joe Biden | 55 |
| What's the Matter With Virginia? | 58 |
| In Front of a Philadelphia Abortion Clinic, Democratic Lawmakers Shows Us the Darkness of the Cultural Divide | 61 |
| Real American Sits at One End of the Potomac–and at the Other | 64 |
| Coming Home | 67 |
| It Can Take a Foreigner to Teach Us the American Dream | 71 |

| | |
|---|---|
| Finding American at a Back-Roads Gas Station | 74 |
| What Happens When Joe Stops Being Joe? | 77 |
| Richard Trumka and Big Labor Try to Come Home | 80 |
| 'Real America' Inside the Beltway | 83 |
| In North Carolina Special, National Questions Intrude on Local Issues | 85 |
| Party, Personality, a Big Name and a Primary in Western Michigan | 88 |
| Lara Trump Tries to fix Her Party's Woman Problem | 91 |
| Rural America, 'Romanticism' and Open Minds | 94 |
| Rats Infest Our Cities, but There Are Bigger Barriers to a Better Life | 97 |
| The Death of a Local Newspaper Rocks America to Its Core | 100 |
| The Perils of Trading Social Interaction for Social Media | 103 |
| Small-Business Men Get a Front-Row Seat for Everyday Life | 106 |
| Cancel Culture Isn't Real Life–Yet | 109 |
| It Will Take Hometown Heroes to Fix Brokem Towns | 112 |
| The Crackers and Frackers Could Hold the Keys to 2020 | 115 |
| Repurposing 'America's Hometown' | 118 |
| Old-School House Democrats Face Primary Challenges From Progressives Across the Country | 121 |
| Our 90-Second Culture | 124 |
| How Small Cities and Towns Can Right Their Ship | 127 |
| Why Mark Zuckerberg Wants to Recruit Outside the Ivy League Liberal Bubble | 130 |
| Will Democrats Miss Middle America Again? | 133 |
| The Bellwether House Race for 2020 Is in Western Pennsylvania | 136 |
| Pennsylvania 2020: It's Complicated | 140 |
| America's Troubled Waters | 143 |
| Dr. Laura's Lasting Truths | 146 |

| | |
|---|---|
| In the 'Nicest Place in America,' Community Thrives | 149 |
| He Makes a Village | 152 |
| A Different Kind of Celebrity on Twitter | 155 |
| The Town That Wouldn't Be Passed By | 158 |
| The Great Revolt Enters a New Phase: How the Populist Uprising of 2016 Will Reverberate in 2020 | 161 |
| About the Author | 165 |

# American Civic Life Tries to Make a Comeback

*January 1, 2019*

PITTSBURGH–It's just before 7 p.m. on a frigid December night, and already the Allegheny Elks Lodge No. 339 on the city's North Side is filling up quickly–both the long bar and the tables in the adjacent hall.

There's a woman collecting for a 50-50 raffle. (You may as well give in; she won't take no for an answer.) Elks volunteers young and old are manning the bar and the kitchen, where the special tonight is a gourmet grilled cheese (black forest honey ham, Gouda cheese and bacon).

Upstairs a six-lane sparkling white and red art deco bowling alley straight out of the 1920s is filled with young people from a local league. The floor above that is where lodge meetings are held; it is a beautiful ballroom also straight out of the Roaring '20s.

The beer is cheap and cold. The food is cheap and tasty. Soon the entire building is packed to the rafters, people lining the walls in the hall and the bar. It's as if Frank Capra made a movie in this century.

Tonight is Banjo Night, the weekly event when the Pittsburgh Banjo Club takes to the stage in the 90-year-old building. The event attracts an eclectic mix of college students; suburbanites; pink-haired, inked, multi-pierced artists; and octogenarians all joining in to sing along to tunes like "Daisy, Daisy" and "You are my Sunshine."

There's even a free song sheet, but it carries a stern warning: "Thou shall not take with you."

This is not an Elks event, as the Banjo Club rents the hall every week. Still, its presence at the lodge has helped reignite interest in the civic organization that first came into being just after the Civil War. A group of young actors initially formed a social club to elude New York City's strict Sunday tavern hours of operation. Theatrical shows would end too late for them to grab a drink after a show.

The Jolly Corks, as they were originally called, evolved into a charitable civic group through tragedy. One of the original members died, leaving his widow and children destitute, and they all chipped in to ease her financial stress. This moment transformed their organization from the social Jolly Corks to the service-oriented Elks.

Memberships in civic organizations such as the Elks or Masons or Rotary Clubs peaked across America after both world wars, and they began falling in the 1960s when Americans began shedding fraternal socialization and front porches for television shows in their living rooms and backyard decks.

Since the late '90s, all of them have rapidly faced near extinction, thanks to the isolating effects of gaming and smartphones, and the anti-social components of social media. These things erase that sense of community, security and civic duty that fraternal organizations can cultivate.

By 2012, the membership at this Elks had hit a low, only 340 members remaining, and most of them were closer in age to 80 than to 70. The community was ebbing in fast-forward, and that social capital was evaporating.

And something else was fading: the tradition of elders sharing stories, sometimes tall tales, passing on their wisdom and experiences to the young people in the community. It's the kind of knowledge and information you can't Google or ask Alexa to find for you, the kind of knowledge that shapes the character of men and women and a community.

Today the membership is nearly double its 2012 low point. Weekly outside events like Banjo Night and the monthly jazz and bluegrass nights bring the crowds. Annual events like the Lenten Fish Fry and the very popular Johnny Cash Night, which always falls on the late crooner's birthday and typically features several Cash cover bands, have raised enough awareness about what Elks actually do that membership has soared.

And the scope of its work, all volunteer, is astounding, from supplementing federal food stamp deficiencies for the local poor, to summer day camps for at-risk kids, to youth drug-awareness programs, to veterans programs, to visiting nurses, to a holiday charity drive.

There was even a luggage charity drive to collect gently used luggage, totes and book bags for foster children transitioning between homes and women transitioning in or out of women's shelters. This provided a bit more dignity than the black trash bag Health and Human Services provides.

They also raised money for the victims of Hurricane Maria in Puerto Rico and for the Tree of Life Synagogue Victims & Families Fund in the aftermath of the mass shooting this fall.

All of these only touch the tip of the iceberg of the philanthropic work this one lodge does, with many of the new members having first walked through the lodge doors on Banjo Night, looking for a place that could become a second home of sorts, a place to connect with people they were somehow missing in their lives.

Too often people think that to make significant change in the world they have to get involved in global issues or lobbying the central government. What they miss is that most things that improve the world begin in a small community civic organization like this Elks– even something like helping homeless veterans get a free haircut, interview clothing and housing until they get on their feet.

That vet or the kid who gets a scholarship through the Elks will in turn keep alive the notion of service and go on to improve the world in his or her own way.

Ray Link, the young "exalted ruler" of this lodge, says there are a dozen or so new members about to be sworn in to this Elks beginning in 2019. Even the mayor of Pittsburgh, Bill Peduto, has been a member in good standing for a couple of years.

Joining has been something Americans have been doing for centuries. In the past decade, we've sadly replaced our participation in churches and civic organizations with a heavy participation in politics and social media, neither of which really does much for us or our communities.

# From Tea Party Insurgent to Last Man Standing: Ron Johnson in Wisconsin

*January 8, 2019*

There is an irony in the fact that Ron Johnson is the guy who will carry the mantle forward for the Republican Party in Wisconsin. Even he admits that.

"I kind of sprang out of the tea party movement and was sort of a grassroots guy," says Sen. Johnson about his entry into politics a decade ago. "First public speech I'd ever given was in October 2009. And people came up to me afterwards and said, 'Hey, I liked your speech. Why don't you run for office?' My reply was always pretty consistent. I said, 'Because I'm not crazy.' Then, they passed Obamacare, and I started thinking about it."

In short order, he entered the Senate race, picked up endorsements from the grassroots and establishment alike, and easily carried the nomination.

Six months later, he was part of a percolating populist conservative movement that swept the Democrats out of power in the formerly blue state. Johnson unseated Democratic Sen. Russ Feingold, and Republican Scott Walker took the governorship from the Democrats, while Republicans took control of both the state Assembly and Senate, held the state attorney general's office, swung the state treasurer's office and took two congressional seats long held by Democrats.

Not long after, Janesville Rep. Paul Ryan would be named chairman of the House Ways and Means Committee and then become the vice presidential nominee. Wisconsin GOP Chairman Reince Priebus would become chairman of the national Republican Party.

Following the 2010 election, Wisconsin's GOP was the beating heart of the national GOP.

Now almost 10 years later, Walker lost his bid for a third term last November; Ryan, who rose to speaker of the House, is now leaving Congress; and Priebus has been chased out of Trump's White House.

That leaves one guy standing to steer the Midwest conservative movement back into power–or at least be the face of it. That is Johnson.

He says of the 2018 midterms: "I went to bed on election night. ... Scott Walker was pulling ahead and just had the out counties, which we normally win. So, I was pretty confident he was going to win, kind of breathed a sigh of relief, never went to sleep. But I got a text. It was called ... for his opponent. One of my first thoughts was, other than the expletive, was 'I am last man standing.' And I have a unique responsibility, which I take seriously."

Johnson says he has Priebus giving him advice on how to reassess the way forward, but he is adamant that returning does not begin or end at the top.

He explained: "The postmortem is that I'm making calls all the time, and we have a pretty robust effort right now. But the feedback is pretty consistent. The campaigns were very top-down, and they weren't listening to people. Long-term volunteers that had worked their tail off for me kind of gave up and said, 'Yeah, it's not worth it.'"

His plan to re-energize the grassroots effort began with him personally calling the county chairmen in the state just before Christmas. "It is important to engage them early and often during this process," he says. "The input is so consistent from what we need to do. I keep referring to it as trickle-up elections. Rather than top-down, all senators talk about one person. I mean, we need to return to the Republican Party of Wisconsin and a party that supports all Republican candidates and helps recruit candidates but supports them in all levels, local, county."

Johnson says in leading the rebuilding, he is going to do what Wisconsin conservatives do well: work together. In short, this state has always been the robust epicenter of the modern populist conservative movement because the establishment, the tea party and talk radio have always avoided the GOP civil wars that have plagued the national scene. Johnson not only gets that; he is banking on that.

His critical test will be the state Supreme Court race in April 2020. "It will occur during the presidential primary, and if we got a nominee and they don't, it's really going to be difficult to win that, and that could flip the court," he says.

Seven months after that first test comes the presidential election. Johnson strikes you as the guy who doesn't want to be the accidental leader of a movement who loses the big game.

# Rick Scott Chased the Hispanic Vote and Got It

*January 15, 2019*

Nine years ago Rick Scott, then a Florida businessman, sat down with a group of self-described jaded Republican strategists to discuss what it would take for him to run for governor.

"You are not going to get anywhere with Hispanic voters, but we'll try," said Wes Anderson, founding partner and pollster for OnMessage Inc. (where my co-author, Brad Todd, works).

"Rick Scott looked at us and just shook his head. He said, 'I reject your dismissal of Hispanic voters. We are going to pursue them, and we're gonna pursue them hard,'" explained Anderson. "He flat-out rejected that there was this big chunk voters that you can just write off and you're never gonna get."

It is a rejection every Republican candidate running for office should emulate.

Scott, who won by two-tenths of a percentage point over incumbent Sen. Bill Nelson, did so despite suffering the same poor performance among suburban voters all Republicans did. He made up for that shortfall with healthy support among Hispanic voters. He won 48 percent of the Hispanic vote, just about the same portion he won in his two gubernatorial victories.

Anderson said OnMessage conducted a post-election survey of 1,014 Hispanic Florida Senate election voters for contemplation: "Every time we win in a state we do a post-elect so that we can figure out what we did right, and what we did wrong, and what we need to do for the future." In an exclusive to the Examiner, OnMessage released the findings of the survey, which was stratified to reflect turnout.

The bilingual telephone interviews were conducted Dec. 10-15 of last year with a margin of error of plus or minus 3 percentage points.

The Hispanic voter breakdown was 35 percent Cuban, 21 percent Puerto Rican and 44 percent other, which includes Colombian, Venezuelan and other South American countries.

The partisan breakdown was 44 percent Democrat, 42 percent Republican and 11 percent independent, with 2 percent refusing to answer.

The first question was "Who is the most popular statewide elected official, Gov. Rick Scott, Sen. Bill Nelson, Sen. Marco Rubio, or President Trump?"

"This is the image test," Anderson said. "The most popular person of the four we tested without question was Rick Scott." Scott topped out at 56 percent, with Nelson and Rubio both at 53 percent and Trump at 45 percent.

On job approval, Scott scored at 61 percent, with 47 percent strongly approving and 14 percent somewhat approving.

"Hispanics, including a chunk who said, 'I'm not sure if I like him personally,' said, 'Yeah, he's doing a good job as governor,'" explained Anderson.

Then the survey asked a series of agree/disagree statements, where surveyors read the voters a question and they answered whether they agree or disagree. On whether Scott cares about the concerns of Hispanic communities in Florida, 58 percent agreed, and 37 percent disagreed.

"Scott blows it out with Cubans, but we had majorities of all Hispanic voters agreeing that yes, Gov. Rick Scott, in fact, cares about the concerns," Anderson said.

The next agree/disagree question on Scott's time as governor of Florida was whether he made it a better place for Hispanics to prosper. Fifty-eight percent agreed, and 35 percent disagreed.

Scott, who was sworn in Tuesday, Jan. 8, talked to the Examiner exclusively about this survey and his early refusal to give up on Hispanic voters.

In his first sit-down interview since becoming senator, Scott said he's never believed people vote just based on the color of their skin.

"I think that their vote is tied to what's in their best interest, as a general rule. And so as governor, what I found is most issues come down to one of three things: They want a job; everybody does. They want their kids to get a good education. And they want to live in a safe community," he said. "And so what I did was I showed up, and I showed up and I talked to everybody."

Scott said he went to Hispanic communities, Hispanic groups and small businesses and focused on their issues "no different than" he focuses on everyone else's. "I put a lot of effort into making sure I could speak Spanish," he said.

What is his message for his fellow Republicans who often struggle with Hispanic voters, especially as the debate in Washington heats up over border security and what to do with illegal immigrants, especially given the sentiments expressed at the end of the survey?

He said: "I think what we have to talk about is what people care about. They care about security. I don't meet people that don't want border security. And I'll talk to anybody, right?"

He added: "People want a secure border, and they want everybody to have the same chance. And we want it to be fair. And I agree with them. And so what we've got to talk about is the dream of this country, which I lived. From public housing, getting to go build companies, being governor now senator. You've gotta talk about, 'I want that for you. And I want that for your children, and I want that for your grandchildren.' And it's gotta be sincere."

Anderson said his biggest takeaway from the survey is that it's a result of eight years of showing up. "That is not six months of showing up. That's eight years of showing up and speaking Spanish the best you can," he said. "You don't get to that level where a Republican sitting governor has 58 percent of Hispanic voters saying that he cares about them without doing that."

# Amtrak Forgot Trains Aren't Planes

*January 22, 2019*

PITTSBURGH–For nearly a quarter of a century, Amtrak's Capitol Limited route has taken me from my beloved hometown to Washington, D.C. Sometimes for fun, almost always for work, the experience is never the same.

And if you are a rail lover, it is always about the experience.

There is only one train that leaves the Pittsburgh station every day, and that is at 5:20 a.m. (which means your alarm goes off at 3:30 a.m.). Thanks to sharing the line with freight, that almost always means a 20- to 90-minute departure delay. Then there's the nearly eight-hour trip, twice what it takes me to drive there. Flying would only take an hour.

So why ride the rails? For starters, there's the joy of looking out your window to swaths of the countryside you'd never see if you were flying over them or cruising along the Pennsylvania Turnpike.

There are miles of old industrial sites in places like Braddock and McKeesport, Pennsylvania, some filled with ghosts of the past. If you are curious enough, you look up what they were as you pass them by and learn something new about the cities and towns that built this country, as well as the people who built it.

You also see a remarkable amount of them being reused or repurposed as new companies chase the ghosts away. Rebirth among the ashes is the story of America.

The post office in Meyersdale, Pennsylvania, is charming. The decay of the old brewery in Smithton, Pennsylvania, is hauntingly beautiful. The rapids of the Youghiogheny in Ohiopyle, Pennsylvania, are breathtaking. So are the sleepy little towns like Hyndman, Pennsylvania, and Paw Paw, West Virginia, where the long-long-short-long warning whistle of the train at each crossing echoes off the mountains that surround these valley towns.

What happens inside the train matters as well. One of the true charming parts of the ride is the dining car experience. It isn't just the warm, buttery grits and the crisp bacon. It is the people you meet because of the communal dining.

It was there on the Friday before former President Barack Obama's first inauguration where I met African-Americans traveling from as far as California by train to attend his inauguration. From veterans of the civil rights movement to young people caught up in his aspirational rhetoric, we were all sitting, conversing, sharing stories and experiences.

Last Monday, when I boarded the train for the first time this winter, I discovered the warm, buttery grits were no longer an option, replaced by a tub of yogurt and granola–in a box. Dinner now came in a box. So did lunch. Gone were the crisp white tablecloths, and gone were the people who always cheerfully made whatever meal you wanted.

My first reaction was: If I were to want to be treated the way I am on an airline, I would take one. I took to Twitter and Facebook to express my disappointment in my best mom tone.

A call to Amtrak at first met deflection. As is the norm with spokesmen these days, they declined to talk and tried to insist I put my questions in email.

However, persistence, done courteously, sometimes does prevail. Apparently, I wasn't the only objector. Amtrak returned to hot meals by this past Wednesday.

The crisp, white tablecloths and the jobs have not returned. In fact, a month ago, employees held a small rally in D.C. to protest the dining service changes and the threat of outsourcing some 1,700 union food and beverage jobs.

Change is inevitable. Change is important. But it is often spurred by erroneous assumptions.

As Peggy Noonan commented on Twitter: "Amtrak's new management thinks trains are planes. A lot of us are on the train because we don't want to be on the plane."

Notably, Amtrak's new president, Richard Anderson, is the former chief executive of Delta Air Lines. There are a lot of things about rail service that can and should be modernized. But there are also some that shouldn't.

Anderson's next course of action should be a trip around the country by rail to listen to his devoted customers and learn who they are and why they ride. He and his team might realize what shouldn't be changed.

# Nostalgia and the American Dream Aren't Airy Fantasies

*January 29, 2019*

BRYAN, Ohio–When the New England Confectionery Co. filed for bankruptcy in Boston last spring, there was such an immediate and deep sense of loss across the country that folks took to local stores and Amazon to claim a piece of yet another what-used-to-be.

Necco Wafers, its signature product, had been part of Americana since before the Civil War. In fact, the company said the sugary, chalky wafers were a favorite of soldiers because the confection didn't melt, and that they were consumed by Union soldiers on the battlefield during the Civil War and by GIs during World War II.

Any Catholic kid of the '60s will tell you it was their parish's practice wafer for the least holy, most worldly part of preparation for first Holy Communion. I never liked them (my dad adores them, in particular the licorice flavor). When I asked Sister Leo if I could pass on the wafer, she allowed it, but only after a lecture in which she said, "You are not going to like the taste of the communion wafer much either, but you don't get to pass on that."

Go on Amazon today and some price points for a bag of Necco Wafers are nearly $60. Why? My guess is the nostalgia they evoke in us about simpler or happier times in our lives or our communities.

Even if in those times, everything around us was, in truth, chaotic, challenging or even awful. Maybe having that wafer reminds of respites we could find.

Nostalgia is a complicated emotion. Initially it raises our endorphins as we flash back and momentarily relive those times. But it also evokes a deep sense of loss because those times and experiences will likely never return. We are completely powerless to change that, and we know it.

Many professionals who live in larger cities and communities and have made the decision to embrace our current culture of dramatic and rapid change with gusto face a complication, their refusal to listen to the people who sometimes want the world to slow down. To them, nostalgia often simply means racism. To many others, though, nostalgia means seeking something that was lost.

The more cosmopolitan class–caught up, living and enjoying societal and political upheaval–too often views those who aren't on board–or who are more nostalgic for a more personally connected society–as less intelligent, backward, bigoted or too tied to the tenets of their faith. These views are not new to the Trump era. They have been building for years and went largely unnoticed–until their class lost a presidential election in 2016.

Why this rejection? The list of reasons is long. In his riveting and important new book, "Alienated America," my Washington Examiner editor, Tim Carney, explores those deeper reasons and unearths the true losses that lie inside that nostalgia.

What cosmopolitan critics have gotten wrong about nostalgia since this populism began is the assumption that it is rooted in racism. They firmly believed then, as they do now, that "Make America Great Again" is code for something nefarious.

Yes, some who were rallied by the MAGA promise were motivated by prejudice and vice–every political movement has its bad travelers. But ask President Trump's earliest supporters and most of them would share a vision of making America great again by rooting it in a wholesome, inclusive vision of the American dream, a dream that was dead or dying for voters in blue-collar communities.

What Carney gets right is that our betters ignored the root of America's angst. Some focused on purely economic decline, but the people living it knew it was cultural collapse. Carney's book digs deeply into that collapse and outlines the decline of America's blue-collar communities, religious institutions and civic institutions that is fraying their bond to one another.

Nostalgia is a big part of America's commerce. It plays a role in fashion and furniture. There is a reason we search for vintage clothing–many spend hours at flea markets or antique stores–and why top-line courtiers look backward for retro designs.

It seems that half of eBay's products are for people looking for something that embodies a time that was.

And sometimes collective nostalgia has power. Here in this northwest Ohio town, 65 miles southwest of Toledo, the Spangler Candy Co., a fairly joyful candy company to visit and home to Dum Dum lollipops, has bought Necco Wafers and Sweethearts and will begin producing them sometime this year.

# Howard Schultz Unifies the Parties– Against Him

*February 6, 2019*

The endless fight between Republicans and Democrats seemed to pause last week.

The cause: former Starbucks CEO Howard Schultz's announcement on "60 Minutes" on Jan. 27 that he is seriously considering a 2020 run for president as a centrist independent. Social media and partisan opinion writers lost their collective minds on that possibility, one of the parties seemingly deploying an activist to disrupt his first public outing, a New York City book event. "Don't help elect Trump, you egotistical billionaire a--hole," the heckler yelled. "Go back to getting ratio'ed on Twitter. Go back to Davos with the other billionaire elites who think they know how to run the world."

The president had his own opinion on a Schultz run, tweeting: "Howard Schultz doesn't have the 'guts' to run for President! Watched him on @60Minutes last night and I agree with him that he is not the 'smartest person.' Besides, America already has that! I only hope that Starbucks is still paying me their rent in Trump Tower!"

The headlines from major newspapers and digital news publications were equally unkind. "Schultz Is the Answer No One Is Looking for" was the CNN headline. Vox went with "Dear Billionaires: Stop Running for President." When "Morning Joe" co-host Mika Brzezinski asked Schultz whether he knows the price of Cheerios, it became a Twitter thing for hours.

The question is: Why the freakout? A Pew survey on political ideology last November showed overall Americans place themselves close to the midpoint on the ideological scale. Why would someone running as a centrist get so much guff?

Easy, said Michael Wear, a Democrat who worked on the White House faith-based initiative during President Barack Obama's first term and directed faith outreach for his 2012 re-election campaign. "I think their position against him goes especially to the early part of the primary process, which is tailored to activists and donors rather than voters, so as someone outside of the party system, they can expose all of those weakness," he said. "And they can also expose all of the room in the middle, because they are trying to win campaigns on how awful the other candidate is."

In short, a Schultz run or any other independent run will expose how the partisan game is played and how much voters' concerns are ignored in favor of donors' and activists'.

Neither party wants to reveal that it wants to avoid the middle to win the primary, and you can't win a primary without throwing red meat to the activists and the donors.

An independent centrist like Schultz wouldn't face the scrutiny of a competitive primary race, said Wear. "That is why I am cold on independent candidacies, especially in an election that is going to be this important."

But that does not mean centrist Democrats shouldn't run. "Of course, there is room for a centrist, and I hope that more centrists run in the Democratic Party," he said, "someone who puts forward an active vision of how government could help those in need, and the crisis we face in economics and climate change, and presses the pause button on the culture wars."

"This is where I think there is an opportunity for someone who would tone down the vitriol in politics and have an active vision to bring us together," said Wear. "I think of Michael Bennet, Mitch Landrieu, John Bel Edwards, or Amy Klobuchar," the Colorado senator, former New Orleans mayor, Louisiana governor and Minnesota senator, respectively.

Every overreaction in American politics tends to be about one of the two parties' vulnerabilities. An independent candidate like Schultz hits both establishment parties' weaknesses; they care more about their donors and their activists than the majority of the people in this country, who is just looking for competent leadership.

# A Surprise Virtual Visit From the President

*February 12, 2019*

WEBSTER SPRINGS, W.Va.–No sitting president has ever visited here before. So it was a pretty big deal when 14 local high school students in a civics class had President Trump talking to them in their classroom Wednesday, all thanks to a Skype video call that Sen. Joe Manchin was having with them.

Senior Brennan Williams, 18, is still grinning ear to ear a few days after the experience. "Well, I mean, I've never talked to somebody that important before, and it was just crazy," he said of initially talking to Manchin. "Then, the president of the United States calls the senator and then decides he wants to talk to us, well, that was even crazier. I just couldn't stop smiling; I still can't."

His classmate Parker Stout, 18, says it was an honor he will never forget: "We prepared for our Skype call with Sen. Manchin by watching the State of the Union Address Tuesday night. What we never expected was that that would include talking to the president."

Manchin said the once-in-a-lifetime event was organized by Webster County High School Principal Stacey Cutlip and his office to discuss issues that came up during the State of the Union address, as well as other topics.

Manchin explained in an interview with the Washington Examiner: "They wanted to talk about the environment. They want to talk about coal, the jobs possibilities, what's going to happen. And they want to talk about guns. As you know, that's usually a big thing. But now the front burner was about the shutdown, how we're going to handle it and border security."

"So, we were talking about all those things, and we were 20 minutes or so into our conversation, and I see on my cellphone 'Unknown' pops up. Well I know the way it pops up, it's either going to be someone from Schumer's office or McConnell's office calling about something," he continued. "Or maybe the White House. You never know."

Turns out it was the White House, specifically, President Trump's assistant.

Manchin told the kids he needed to put them on pause for a few minutes, and all Stout and Williams saw from their vantage point, they explained, was a black screen. A few moments later, Manchin came back and told the students he had "a little surprise" for them.

Manchin put the phone on speaker, and the president started to chat with the kids.

Stout said: "Not everybody in the room you know is politically for Trump, but in that moment that didn't matter, just that fact that you're going to listen to the president talk to a small group of kids. Everyone had a smile on their face and was just so surprised and couldn't really say anything. We just listened to him and smiled."

Manchin said Trump was very charming with the kids: "He says, 'I love West Virginia. And I know they like Joe, and they like me, and we're gonna work together.' And he told them to stay involved, and he appreciates they were very much interested and excited that they were involved in the process and wanted to know what's going on."

The president also mentioned the reason he called Manchin was to thank him for applauding when few Democrats did during bipartisan moments in the State of the Union speech.

Manchin said of his personal conversation with the president: "I said, 'Mr. President, I've always stated that I know my state well and that it's something that my state and I represent the people of my state, I'm going to stand up and be respectful. When I thought the things that you were saying resonated with something I might believe in but definitely my state supports, I'm gonna be there and show the courtesy and manners that I think that I was raised with."

The former governor stood several times and applauded during the president's speech, in particular on energy projects and banning late-term abortions.

Energy's a big thing that Trump talked about, said Manchin. "He didn't talk about coal, but he talked about energy in general," he said. "We're an energy state, and we want to continue to make sure we provide the energy the country needs."

Manchin said the most "controversial" things he applauded were the personal issues on life. He "could ... feel the daggers" when he stood up for Trump's remarks calling for legislation to curb third-trimester abortions. "Late-term abortions, my goodness. It would have to be a dire medical situation," he said, adding that what Virginia Gov. Ralph Northam has supported and what New York Gov. Andrew Cuomo has done with late-term abortion bills in their states is "just totally unconscionable" to him.

Manchin said he was a little struck by the photo on Reuters.com taken of him standing during the speech with Rep. Alexandria Ocasio-Cortez sitting behind him, giving him the stink eye: "My goodness. Well, I could hear the boos a little bit, you know. I didn't know if the boos were for the president or for me standing; I wasn't sure. But I could sure feel the daggers."

Stout said one of the things he really respected about Manchin during the president's speech was how he conducted himself: "That's one thing I really enjoyed watching was he didn't agree with everything that the president said, but things he agreed with, he did stand up. Unlike the other Democrats who didn't, which it's just being partisan over things that can be good for every state."

Stout is heading to West Virginia University in Morgantown, West Virginia, this fall for a degree in criminology, and ultimately, law school. He registered as an independent when he turned 18 late last fall.

Williams is also registered as an independent. He is heading to Fairmont State University for aerospace engineering.

Principal Cutlip said too many people want to put a political spin on the moment; she insisted they are missing the larger point: "Honest to goodness, it really was just we were at the right place at the right time. And I think we were just completely honored that the president did take time out of his day to say hi to the kids. It was just an honor."

Webster Springs, a charming little town located on the Elk River, is a sparsely populated county seat (under 800 people) in a sparsely populated county (under 9,000) where half of the geography is taken up by the majestic beauty and dense forests of the Monongahela National Forest and the Holly River State Park.

Webster County has been a reliable Democratic vote since the state was formed in 1860–data compiled by Dave Leip at Atlas of U.S. Presidential Elections shows that the streak has been broken only three times since then. Webster narrowly went for Richard Nixon in 1972, for Mitt Romney in 2012 (it had gone for Barack Obama in 2008) and for Donald Trump in 2016.

There is no evidence a sitting U.S. president has ever visited the county.

Its economy has relied on coal for over 100 years. As it has declined and devastated the area economically in the past 10 years, shale, the distribution of natural gas through the Mountain Valley Pipeline and tourism have somewhat helped stabilize the slide.

# The Populist Sledgehammer Kills Amazon Jobs that Middle America Would Love to Have

*February 19, 2019*

YOUNGSTOWN, Ohio–Tito Brown can't imagine driving a perfectly good thing out of a town that hasn't had a perfectly good thing come its way in a very long time.

At least, a perfectly good thing the size and scope of the Amazon headquarters that ideological politics drove out of Long Island City on Thursday, when Democrats, including Rep. Alexandria Ocasio-Cortez, danced on the grave of the deal as Amazon walked away from the New York project.

Brown doesn't really get that. He governs a city with a declining population and a 40 percent poverty rate, and he would welcome the opportunity of a project such as Amazon locating here.

"Oh, any time I can get regional and/or economic growth in my community, I would absolutely want that here," he said. "It's budget time."

Ocasio-Cortez, who has become the leader of the left-wing insurgency within the Democratic Party, slammed the plan in a tweet the moment it was announced in mid-November last year.

She initially said the response to the Amazon announcement from her constituents was outrage, arguing that the tax breaks Amazon would receive should be spent by city and state officials on the subway system and communities instead of billion-dollar corporations.

Which isn't how tax breaks work. It's not like there is a pile of money they would hand to Amazon that could have been spent on the subway system, but that is a story for a different day.

What this moment signifies in the Democratic Party is one that has been in existence for several years, but the party establishment and ruling class have been unwilling to face: the leftist populism punching up to take the reins of the party.

New York took a big lurch left last year in the midterm elections when they gave the Democrats their largest majority in the state senate ever, as well as giving Ocasio-Cortez her victory over a moderate establishment Democrat for his Bronx seat in the primary race.

National Democrats hailed the wave and felt empowered, but no one felt more empowered than their left flanks. What the ruling class of the Democratic Party failed to realize is their voters with the largest megaphone believe they are entitled to use it like a sledgehammer, a sledgehammer they plan to use to impact the country's societal, economic and political viewpoints.

Sledgehammers make great copy on Twitter, but they don't help legislators govern, or help job creation–just the opposite.

In New York, the populist sledgehammers cost the region well-paid jobs that ran the gamut from working-class to high-tech. The Amazon project actually enjoyed broad support, with a poll showing as recently as last week that 56 percent of New Yorkers support the project over just 36 percent who do not. Support for it was even higher among minority registered voters than white voters.

In Youngstown, Brown has to govern knowing the possible downfalls that come with large companies locating in communities. But he also knows the upsides. He'd like the upside.

"I think the negatives would be it's a new industry. People are afraid of the change," he said. "It's that 'not in my backyard thing,' but the plus, if I'm those individuals who are underemployed or unemployed, is here's a great opportunity for this great company and it gives them another edge and/or opportunity to advance their family to another level."

At the beginning of the 19th century, an industrial revolution changed this sleepy valley along the Mahoning River from a farming and gristmill community to a manufacturing giant that built the buildings, roads and bridges of the country and lasted for more than 100 years.

People faced change when steel production took over the rivers for commerce, and people faced change when they left.

"We lost our identity of being a steel mill town. That's not coming back. The way we knew life back then, it's not going to happen. There's not going to even be a small glimmer of that life as we knew it then," Brown said. "You talk about the new technology, the new advances that we have coming in the next 10 to 30, 40 years, that's what is happening."

Brown is part of the Democratic Party that is pragmatic on business because he knows business means jobs and jobs mean stability in the community.

"You can't be shortsighted and look at who's delivering the product versus who's actually going to benefit from this product being in your community. It's not poisoning your community. We have a 40 percent poverty rate here in the city of Youngstown. It's probably 85-95 percent of the community is on free and reduced lunch. ... I want to reduce that and eliminate that as the mayor of the city of Youngstown," he said.

Brown said he would be happy to talk to Amazon about locating their headquarters there. With Youngstown's access to the major interstates, close proximity to D.C., New York, Cleveland, Chicago and Pittsburgh, as well as plenty of acreage along the Mahoning River and a solid workforce, he has a strong argument.

People keep sending a message to Washington with their votes, and Washington keeps misreading it. Brown knows why he is the mayor of Youngstown: to create jobs and bring new innovative commerce here, even if that change makes people initially uncomfortable.

It's part of why he, too, upended an incumbent Democrat in a primary election when he won office in 2017.

Ocasio-Cortez seems to have taken the message that her election was a moment for leftist populism, and she is happy to enforce it. If that starts to hurt her district's bottom line, she has a problem. But if it speeds up the spread of leftist populism across the country, it will be interesting to see how that impacts her party and our economy.

## While National Media Carried Water for Jussie Smollett, Local Media Did It Right

*February 26, 2019*

CHICAGO–The first thing that caused newsman Rafer Weigel to blink when reading the TMZ report on "Empire" actor Jussie Smollett being brutally attacked by Trump-supporting, noose-wielding, racial-slurring assailants was the neighborhood in which the attack was reported to have happened.

The Streeterville neighborhood is not exactly "MAGA country" at any time, let alone 2 a.m.

"It is our job as reporters to be skeptical," said Weigel, a local Fox affiliate news anchor and reporter who grew up in Chicago.

How skeptical? "Well as the old adage goes, 'If your mother says she loves you, check it out,' so from the get go, when we heard this about Smollett, there were eyebrows raised for a whole host of reasons, just because we know the city well," he said.

As national media often omitted "alleged" from their reporting of the attack and instead saying that Smollett was attacked by two MAGA hat-wearing people who were "yelling out racial and homophobic slurs" and "poured an unknown chemical substance on the victim," the newsroom Weigel works in, along with several other competing Chicago print and media organizations, mostly stuck "alleged" in their reporting.

Local news organizations were doing what local news organizations do best: staying in constant contact with the local police, local officials and the community, and pursing the past behavior of the victim to look for additional red flags before going in head first with a narrative.

A news organization's relationship with the police, local officials and the community is critical, Weigel said, explaining that as a local news reporter, you often have to report on things that aren't favorable to the community or a local official or the police force. "But because you build trust by being honest and not sensational, those relationships remain intact," he said.

Weigel said the newsroom worked as a team, with people working the phones and talking to detectives in person, often receiving certain information off the record that the detectives would not share with the public because it could compromise their investigation. "So we honor that in order to keep that relationship open." He added: "We have to have good relationships with police officers and local officials, or they will completely cut us off. It is a two-way street. If they have a crime that needs to get solved, they'll turn to us to bring awareness to it, to get out suspects' pictures and videos and that sort of thing. If there's a high-profile case that's of high interest to the public, they understand that, and they will tell us what we can, or what they can, without compromising the investigation. So, it is a two-way street."

As any good local news reporter knows, those working relationships are critical. At the same time, it doesn't mean reporters don't hold them accountable. When there was evidence of a police cover-up of the 2014 shooting of Laquan McDonald by a police officer, the local Chicago media broke the story. The officers involved ended up going to trial. While they were acquitted, the police understand reporters have a job to do. As Weigel said: "We work in close proximity with these people. We know them by their first name, and so therefore, the local media will always have an advantage over the national media swooping in at the last minute, because we already know these people."

National news organizations, the ones with the most Twitter followers or influence on social media, cannot possibly work those kinds of relationships in a meaningful way. But many of them let the story stand without using "alleged" in their reporting, often retweeting celebrities, presidential candidates and influencers who personally condemn the attack, rather than prefacing the attack as an alleged attack.

That kind of omission, including any inference used in the delivery of a story, is damaging to our credibility as dispassionate deliverers of the news.

That behavior is not one a local news reporter can entertain.

On a national level, it took seconds for the story to become that Smollett was a victim of a hate crime, and that once again, supporters of President Trump are racist homophobes who are out for blood. It just stood there for weeks, getting spread by Hollywood, social media and conversations offline. Like so many other false stories recklessly spread, it became an axiom.

Except it wasn't.

The most important lesson of this debacle is not that national news is bad but that local news matters at the very same time it is dying.

It is a death that does no one good, certainly not the cities and towns and municipalities that need someone holding their water authorities, school boards, police officers, mayors and city councils in check.

We need them to cover the abuses of power, corruption, and dark secrets and associations that lurk in their past. We need them to follow the money.

Newsroom employment across the country has bottomed out at local newspapers, according to a Pew Research Center analysis of Bureau of Labor Statistics Occupational Employment Statistics. Its survey data shows a 23 percent job loss in local news from 2008 to 2017.

We need more reporters like Rafer Weigel. We need more reporters like the ones I used to work with in Pittsburgh. But there is no quick fix, or perhaps any fix, to this crisis. Technology has changed the media industry.

Like any industry changed by automation, the horse is out of the barn.

## Trump's Anti-Socialist Strength Could Turn Venezuelan-Americans Into Republicans for Decades

*March 5, 2019*

MIAMI–Ernesto Ackerman watched the horror in Venezuela play out on a large screen onstage at a rally he helped organize in support of the country's opposition leader, Juan Guaido. The event was initially meant to bring Venezuelans in the city together to coincide with the protests back home. It ended up being something very different.

"A killing of civilians without arms, burning the humanitarian help. We are dealing with the genocide," the Venezuelan-American activist said as they watched the violence play out in real time.

Ackerman, a medical equipment sales executive and co-founder of the nonpartisan grassroots organization Independent Venezuelan-American Citizens, was referring to the Venezuelan border standoff led by President Nicolas Maduro that not only prohibited the much-needed food and medical humanitarian aid meant for the Venezuelan people to enter the country but also resulted in the death of four people.

Guaido, the leader of the National Assembly, swore himself in as interim president of Venezuela in January, challenging Maduro, who has led the country since 2013. The U.S., along with scores of other countries, recognized Guaido as the leader, and Venezuela's citizens have taken to the streets to protest the nation's ravaging poverty and economic collapse under Maduro.

Those clashes between opposition protesters and forces loyal to Maduro escalated during the attempted delivery of humanitarian supplies. They came exactly one week after President Trump spoke at Florida International University, saying that the U.S. stands with the Venezuelan people and against socialism.

"We seek a peaceful transition of power, but all options are open," Trump said in a dramatic speech to a crowd of supporters including Ackerman, who had his picture taken with the president after the speech.

On Monday, Vice President Mike Pence spoke to the Lima Group of nations in Bogota, Colombia, reinforcing the administration's position that the U.S. has Guaido's back.

The Trump administration upped the pressure by giving more than $50 million in additional aid to Venezuela's neighboring countries to provide safety to Venezuelan refugees, as well as announcing more sanctions against backers of Maduro.

It is exactly what Ackerman and other Venezuelan-Americans want to hear for their former countrymen who live in poverty and fear there. Ackerman's mother, a 96-year-old Slovenian, was in the Auschwitz concentration camp. "She is saying that she lives again in a concentration camp," said Ackerman of her life now. Ackerman's brother, a lawyer by trade, has cancer and hasn't been able to work for years. "He cannot work. There is no courts working, nothing," said Ackerman.

Ackerman is a supporter, not just of President Trump's strong position on the Maduro government but also of the president himself.

"I am a Republican. I cannot understand anyone who has come from Venezuela who would be anything else," he said, adding that what made him a Republican was the idea he could achieve whatever he wanted on his own.

He said of his successes since arriving here in the late 1980s: "Yesterday, we had a meeting with the businessmen from Venezuela. And I explained to them, when I left Venezuela, I wanted–my dream was to be a millionaire, to have a big house, to have a nice car. And that's what democracy and the Republican Party's giving me."

Ackerman is part of an earlier wave of Venezuelan immigrants, many of whom are organizing to help the thousands of new Venezuelans who have been pouring into our country in recent years to flee overwhelming economic collapse and political strife. According to the nonpartisan Migration Policy Institute, immigration from Venezuela has increased by 21 percent between 2016 and 2017 and almost doubled since 2010.

Like the Cubans who came before them who felt betrayed by the Democratic Party during the Cuban missile crisis, Venezuelan voters are moving their loyalty toward the Republican Party because of its strong stance against socialism and communism.

Ackerman said: "Most of the Venezuelans are Democrats. And I really don't understand why. Now, saying that, I see like in maybe in the last year–I see a lot of these Democrats being now pro-President Trump. They know what socialism is. They fled the results of that. They are now seeing all the opportunity and freedom that comes with capitalism, and they are moving that way."

In a state where elections are decided by a slim margin, both parties are always looking to win over new constituencies. Ackerman is convinced Republicans are building an edge, not just on how they treat small businesses–which he says a majority of Venezuelans start once they come to this country–but also on foreign policy.

"If President Trump is persuasive in having Maduro step aside, I think Venezuelan-Americans can be loyal to Republicans for many years to come," said Ackerman.

"When (Trump) said, 'This will be the only region in the world that is not going to have socialism, and the United States won't be socialist either,'" explained Ackerman "that was a very powerful message to everybody."

# Losing a Hometown Hero

*March 12, 2019*

PITTSBURGH–Baseball is always held up as a metaphor for life in America. The struggles and disappointments, along with the workaday perseverance, form clear parallels.

Both require hope.

Baseball historian David Pietrusza once told me that like baseball, America is all about hope, necessarily tied up with effort and disappointment.

Baseball is a game without a clock. It's never over until the final out. And no matter what the score is, there's always a chance. Hope is the 10th guy in every lineup.

Like many traditions in American life that have changed with the times–such as knowing you can stay and prosper in the same town that your father's father's father did–the idea that your favorite player will be in the outfield playing for your home team his entire career is also a thing of the past.

Brad Todd lives in the Washington area, and his 9-year-old son's favorite player, Bryce Harper, just traded his Washington Nationals jersey for a Philadelphia Phillies jersey and a $330 million contract. This brings back memories for Todd.

"I can remember the date, the day and where I was," he said, a lifelong Atlanta Braves fan and co-author of our book, "The Great Revolt." "It was August the 3rd, 1990. I was a college student working a summer job at a newspaper, and I remember when, all the sudden, I saw it pop up on my screen that Dale Murphy had been traded, ironically, to the Philadelphia Phillies, and I looked up and everyone in the newsroom was staring at me. They had already seen it and were waiting on my reaction."

But the situation is worse for his son.

He said, "Murphy was at the end of his career. And so I still knew that he would be a Braves legend, and not somebody else's legend. And that's the problem I think with Harper. These kids thought that he would play for their team forever, and now he's going to end up spending the bulk of his career playing for their rivals." The Phillies and the Nats are both in the National League East division.

Since free agency came about in the '70s, it has been a mournful rite of passage for young and old fans. This paralleled the broader phenomenon of more Americans leaving the place they grew up and thought they'd stay, having either been pulled away by opportunity, or pushed out by automation or foreign competition.

George Will, the Washington Post columnist who wrote the book on baseball "Men at Work," says free agency may be one of the best things that happened to baseball. He explained in an interview: "It has, after much tweaking and accommodations, I think, contributed a competitive balance. It has made baseball more interesting. But even if it had done neither, it would be a good idea, because it's elemental justice that the reserve clause denied. Which is the basic American right to negotiate terms of employment with the employer of your choice."

Will, who saw his first game at Forbes Field here in Pittsburgh, knows there are plenty of 9-year-old broken hearts across the country every time this happens. "What we learn about baseball is that people are loyal less to particular players and more to the uniform and the logo and the stadium and the whole thing that goes with a team," he says.

This is likely why in culture, you find loyalty to hometowns in other cities in the most peculiar ways. For instance, the 1,500 Steelers bars that are located across the country provide a way to connect what was lost after thousands and thousands of families were forced to leave when manufacturing collapsed here in the 1970s.

Washington is a jaded city. The adults are going be disappointed but not surprised, and will move past it. But in the end, baseball is a game that lives mostly in the imaginations of little kids and the little kid in all of us. And for that little kid, the loss of a lefty slugger is a little taste of the common sad story of losing hometown things we love.

# From the Rubble of a Church Rises a Spirit of Love

*March 19, 2019*

COLUMBUS, Miss.–At the First Pentecostal Church on Tuscaloosa Road, the last Saturday of February was a day filled with supposed-to-be's.

Little Jereson McCool was supposed to be at the church hall surrounded by 60 members of his family and community to celebrate his fifth birthday, but his grandma's train from South Carolina was running five hours late. His mom, Misty, made the call from the train station to the church's Pastor Steve Blaylock to see whether they could move it to the next day.

Tom and Betty Lindsay, an elderly couple who live by the river, were supposed to hole up in a residence located in the church because of pending flooding, but Betty's sister insisted instead that they stay at her home 20 miles away.

The mother-daughter cleaning crew that was supposed to be cleaning the sanctuary of the church for the big baptismal service that was planned for the next day decided at the last minute to just go do it early in the morning.

These last-minute changes to plans proved to be lifesavers. A tornado–one of nine that ravaged parts of Alabama, Georgia and here in Mississippi–destroyed the very church building they would have been in, ripping off the roof and collapsing the walls. A few untouched pews remained as a reminder that a house of God once stood there.

"Even in the midst of all that destruction, there was so many miracles, things that just are unexplainable that happened, that only God could cause," said Blaylock. The pastor's voice cracked as he considered the lives that would have been lost. When he drove up the road and saw the structural devastation of his church, he felt profound gratitude that none of those people who were supposed to be there were there.

The violent tornado leveled 300 homes, closed down the local school and cost one person her life. It also brought the community and strangers together the next morning to begin rebuilding the structure and renewing faith.

"As we were trying Saturday evening to get anything out of the Sanctuary that we could recover, we started talking about what are we gonna do about church tomorrow," Blaylock said. "So I started asking you know, maybe we oughta wait until another Sunday to do our Baptismal service rather than the next day. One particular man, Blake Brown, told us that if there's any way possible, I still wanna get baptized. He was new to our church, and boy, that just excited me and everybody else. We're like, we'll make it happen. We'll make it happen, if we have to go to the river or whatever we do, we'll make it happen."

So they did. The miraculous thing was that people came. People came from their church, and locals who didn't belong to the church came. Strangers who just happened to hear about what happened came.

"Obviously, we have been a greater light in our community than what we realize," Blaylock said.

First Pentecostal, unlike some Southern Pentecostal churches, is not divided by race. Both blacks and whites practice in a town whose population is 63 percent black and 35 percent white.

It is also a Democrat town in a Republican state.

"There are so many forces in our world that divide people," Blaylock said. "But to see the community in our area, we are a mixed community. We have Hispanics, we have Native Americans, we have blacks, we have white, we have mixes of all kinds. But everybody, everybody was out helping each other."

He added, "Nobody asked what political party that you supported while we were out there Saturday night and Sunday. Nobody cared who was beside them, they were just thankful that they were there, and that they were helping, and they expressed love."

That Sunday morning, the day after the tornado hit, a total of nine people were baptized in an outdoor service using a borrowed baptism tank. Two hundred attendees sat in folding chairs surrounded by jagged lumber. Two hundred people showed up to dig them out so they could have their service.

Even the local Lowe's showed up with a flatbed, bottles of water and dozens of work gloves to lend a hand.

Blacklock said, "Our motto before the storm was, 'Loving God and Loving People.' And now our motto is, 'To Rebuild Bigger and Stronger Together.' Might not be bad a motto for the whole country."

## Beto O'Rourke: Late-term Abortions Are 'About Women Making Their Own Decisions About Their Own Body'

*March 26, 2019*

STATE COLLEGE, Pa.–Beto O'Rourke has refused to rule out abortions more than six months into a pregnancy.

Asked by the Washington Examiner about his stance on third-trimester abortions, O'Rourke, who's battling with a crowded field of Democrats vying for the chance to unseat President Trump in 2020, said it is a woman's decision, in consultation with her doctor.

"Listen, I think those decisions are best left to a woman and her doctor," he said. "I know better than to assume anything about a woman's decision, an incredibly difficult decision, when it comes to her reproductive rights."

He added: "Roe v. Wade, though it is being tested unlike any other time, is still the law of the land. It must be upheld, and we must ensure that when we are talking about universal health care, we are also talking about women's health care. And when we are talking about women's health care, we are talking about women making their own decisions about their own body."

O'Rourke was being asked to clarify comments he made in Cleveland the night before in response to a woman asking him whether he supports third-trimester abortions. The woman noted that in those cases, the fetus might be viable outside of the womb, and if there were an emergency, doctors could perform a cesarean section.

He answered the woman's question quickly, not addressing the root of the inquiry but simply saying that he supports a woman's right to an abortion.

He told her: "So, the question is about abortion and reproductive rights. And my answer to you is that should be a decision that the woman makes. I trust her."

While 6 in 10 Americans broadly support abortion rights for the first trimester, a Gallup poll from last June said that number drops to 13 percent in the final three months of a pregnancy.

O'Rourke, 46, a former Texas congressman who announced his presidential run March 14, said it was important to visit Pennsylvania, Wisconsin, Michigan and Ohio right out of the gate, an implicit criticism of defeated 2016 Democratic nominee Hillary Clinton, who neglected the Rust Belt and lost all four states.

"The places that I visited are really important to me. I want to make sure that we are not writing anyone off, and just as importantly, I want to make sure we are not taking anyone for granted," he said. "When we don't show up, we get what we deserve. When we don't show up, we fail to learn from those we fail to serve."

Clinton was widely panned for ignoring Wisconsin and Michigan until the end of the campaign.

"If we have any hope of winning, and if we have any prospect of delivering, we have to first show up with the humility of acknowledging that," O'Rourke said as he walked along Pollock Road with 20 members of the Penn State College Democrats.

O'Rourke spent a half-hour with the student activists at the Nittany Lion statue, taking questions about college tuition and taking photos with the group.

Donning a white Penn State hat, O'Rourke even learned the finer details of the iconic "We are ... Penn State!" chant that typically echoes out of Beaver Stadium during football season.

O'Rourke represented El Paso, Texas, for six years in the House before challenging incumbent Republican Sen. Ted Cruz for his Senate seat in 2018. Despite the long odds–the last Democrat to win a U.S. Senate seat in Texas was Democratic Sen. Lloyd Bentsen in

1988, when he won re-election for a fourth term—he made it a race, coming within 2.6 percentage points of Cruz.

Of the candidates who have announced or are considering a run, O'Rourke is the youngest. On March 18, he announced that his campaign brought in $6.1 million in the first 24 hours, outraising everyone in the field, including Vermont Sen. Bernie Sanders, who hit $6 million in his first 24 hours.

He broke the fundraising record books last year in Texas, raising over $80 million, more than twice as much as Cruz did.

Charlie Gerow, a Pennsylvania-based Republican media consultant, said O'Rourke was less quixotic than his Democratic critics claim and his Republican rivals wish he was. Gerow said, "Look, he is charismatic in a presidential field vying to show their presidential timber."

O'Rourke was smart to bookend Wisconsin, Michigan, Ohio and Pennsylvania between the traditional early states of Iowa and New Hampshire, Gerow said: "The Rust Belt is going to determine who the next president is and this is ground zero. Right now he is the talk of the town and he has pushed the other Democrats off the front page."

But he added that the only candidate to ever knock everyone off the front pages and stay there for four years is Trump: "Whether O'Rourke can go toe-to-toe with Donald Trump is another story."

# Blue-Collar Worker Bashed by Trump, Wooed by Beto O'Rourke in Same Week

*April 2, 1029*

 LORDSTOWN, Ohio–No one exemplifies the spirit of American manufacturing more than United Auto Workers Local 1112 President David Green.

 Charismatic, humble and a relentless optimist, he is the everyman who guys like Bruce Springsteen and Billy Joel wrote ballads about in the 1980s.

 But Green also has to face a triple whammy: shifting consumer taste, the callousness of big business and the manipulations of politicians–the same factors that have dogged American car manufacturing since the first assembly line started at Ford Motors in December 1913.

 It's a burden he doesn't take lightly. And in 2019, it comes with the added pressure of the president of the United States publicly accusing him of failure.

 "Democrat UAW Local 1112 President David Green ought to get his act together and produce," President Trump tweeted March 17. "Stop complaining and get the job done!"

 Green was driving home after a segment on Fox News when a union member called and told him about the tweet.

 "I was a little taken back," he chuckled.

 But he decided not to respond, to set an example.

"If I'm the type of person that's going to lash out and have a nasty reaction, then my kids are going to be that way," he said.

It's been three weeks since the last Chevy Cruze rolled off the plant here in Trumbull County after GM announced it was ending production of its compact car. The plant's imminent closure comes less than 10 years after GM got $50.2 billion in government bailouts following the global economic collapse of 2008.

A loss of over 1,600 plant jobs and almost 3,000 jobs in the regional economy tells just part of the story. The total negative impact is estimated at $3 billion in economic output, according to a study by Cleveland State University's Center for Economic Development.

It is a catastrophic event in an area that is still reeling from decades of economic devastation.

Green is one of the fewer than 200 remaining workers in the 6.2 million-square-foot plant making service parts like hoods, doors and fenders for Cruze vehicles that are still on the road.

"We are making a stockpile of those spare parts," he said. "They anticipate every week laying off what's left of us little by little till just a handful are left to keep the lights on."

Meanwhile, politicians eager to woo the American blue-collar worker are at his doorstep.

Two days after Trump issued his tweet, Democratic candidate Beto O'Rourke sent Green a text.

Green's first thought? "What's a Beto?"

Later that day, O'Rourke met Green at the union hall and afterward called him "a true leader" at a rally in State College, Pennsylvania.

Green said Beto is "nice" and "down-to-earth" but that, like lots of people across the country, he's tired of pandering politicians.

"Politicians, they pull on us from every direction," Green said. "They pull, pull, pull, and all they want is our vote. I hate the negative. I want to see politicians who put up a plan. President Trump, I mean, I think his plan is to win the 24-hour news cycle, and I think he's genius at it. I think he does a fantastic job at that."

Recently, Trumbull County has liked whatever Trump has been saying to win the 24-hour news cycle. After voting for Barack Obama in 2012, it flipped an astonishing 30 percentage points to vote Trump in 2016.

Meanwhile, as Green sat in the union hall, Trump was just three hours away at a manufacturing center in Lima, Ohio, which got a huge boost this year in the defense budget, saving over 1,000 jobs.

During Trump's visit, his mind was still on Lordstown.

"What's going on with General Motors?" he asked the crowd. "Sell it to somebody" or reopen it, he said. "Get it open now. Don't wait."

A rumor rippled through the union hall that Trump might stop in Lordstown, but it never happened.

Green, though, is not deterred: "My sole mission is to get a new car allocated for Lordstown. That means keeping the workers and community engaged and a conversation continuing with GM."

"And to remain optimistic," he added. "This isn't just about preserving jobs. People forget how proud we are of the product we made. When a Cruze drives past me on the street, I look at that and say, 'We made that.'"

If the plant closes permanently after the last spare part is boxed up, Green, 49, plans to take a transfer and retire in five years.

But until then, he will fight on, battling the forces that have always tangled the American worker.

"There is still dignity and hard work in America," Green said. "That's what we stand for here. That is what we are fighting to hold on to. It is the most American thing we can do."

## How Pete Buttigieg Could Hurt Trump in the Rust Belt

*April 9, 2019*

Pete Buttigieg is many things.

At just 37, he is the mayor of South Bend, Indiana. He is a military veteran and a deeply religious gay man who is married but also enjoys sandwiches from (anti-same-sex marriage) Chick-fil-A. He is a Harvard-educated Rhodes scholar who speaks eight languages. He is the first ever millennial candidate for president and, so far, the only Democratic hopeful to appear on the "Fox News Sunday" show.

"I'm all of those things," said Buttigieg–pronounced "Boot-edge-edge"–in an interview with the New York Post. "I try not to have any kind of attribute ... be totally defining," he added.

Critics say these attributes are the very reasons why he can't beat Donald Trump. His supporters say they are the very reasons he can.

Mayor Pete, as he likes to be called, strikes a tone that is kinder and less combative than the insult-driven politics of Trump and the Democratic Party's far-left members. His boyish good looks, intelligence and military background are undoubtedly appealing, as is his faith.

"Scripture tells us to look after the least among us, that it also counsels humility and teaches us about what's bigger than ourselves," said Buttigieg, a devout Episcopalian. "It points the way toward an inclusive and unselfish politics that I strive to practice, whether I'm talking about my faith on the stump or not."

Mayor Pete's politics are already gaining traction. Since launching his exploratory committee to run for president on Jan. 23, he has already raised $7 million for his campaign. A recent Quinnipiac poll found that 4 percent of Democrats would vote for him–the same number that supports Elizabeth Warren, who has been a U.S. senator for six years.

The fact that he was born and bred in the American Rust Belt is possibly his biggest asset.

"Our party can and should do better in the industrial Midwest," Buttigieg said. "I'm convinced that so many people in this part of the country are already with us, much more than with the other party on issues, on substance, on policy."

He said his experience in his hometown of South Bend proves there are solutions that work besides a "promise to turn back the clock."

When Buttigieg was first elected to office in South Bend in 2011, the city was on its knees. Job growth was nonexistent, and like many Rust Belt cities with declining industry, it had been hemorrhaging jobs since the '70s.

First, he improved the cosmetics of the town by demolishing more than 1,000 abandoned homes, and then he focused on revitalizing it by attracting hundreds of millions in private investment for commercial development.

You won't find Buttigieg ridiculing fellow Midwestern voters or taking them for granted, the way Hillary Clinton's campaign did in 2015. After the University of Notre Dame, based in South Bend, invited her to attend their prestigious St. Patrick's Day event, her campaign declined, telling organizers that "white Catholics were not the audience she needed to spend time reaching out to," as The New York Times wrote.

Trump would go on to win those white Catholic votes in 2016–52 percent of them, according to Pew's exit polls, reversing the gains Democrats made when Barack Obama earned their votes in 2008 and 2012.

Even so, Buttigieg's religious beliefs haven't prevented him from taking progressive positions on major issues.

He supports abortions into the third trimester out of a belief in "freedom from government," he said. And he won't rule out tax hikes. "If the only way I can get all of us paid parental leave, universal health care, dramatically improved child care, better education, good infrastructure and, therefore, longer life expectancy and a healthier economy is to raise revenue, then we should be honest about that," he said.

And although natural gas leads to good, solid jobs in the Rust Belt, he is a big booster of wind and solar power. "I think the goal still has to be focused on renewables," he said.

But just because Buttigieg has a progressive platform doesn't mean he'll get an easy ride from far-left Democrats. Last month, the woke crowd at Slate questioned the young mayor's credentials with a since-changed headline that read "Is Pete Buttigieg just another white male candidate, or does his gayness count as diversity?"

And just because Buttigieg is from the Rust Belt doesn't mean he can win a general election in places like Ohio, Michigan, Wisconsin and Pennsylvania, especially when you compare his platform to Trump's.

"He has to share their values on bread-and-butter issues like lower taxes, regulations and religious liberty," warned Dr. G. Terry Madonna, director of the Center for Politics and Public Affairs at Franklin & Marshall College. If he doesn't, "it would be very difficult for him to win."

But Jeff Rea, a former Republican mayor from another Indiana town and current president of the South Bend chamber of commerce, said nobody should count out Mayor Pete. He and Buttigieg have been on opposite sides on a number of projects but have "always found a way to come together for a solution."

Buttigieg "is a very data-driven guy and also a very good man," Rea added. "That has helped him win over voters who might not like progressive politics."

No mayor in history has ever run and won his or her party's nomination for president, nor has anyone under the age of 43. Then again, no businessman had ever done it until Trump came along.

Michael Wear, the faith adviser to Obama, told me he thinks Mayor Pete has a chance.

"Things change," Wear said. "And, in America, anything can happen."

# An Answer to the Cost of College and Community Collapse: Community Colleges

*April 16, 2019*

PITTSBURGH–When the Pittsburgh Pirates opened their season two weeks ago at PNC Park, Nathan Sibley, a York County, Pennsylvania, kid who struggled in high school and subsequently stood little chance to attend a four-year college had earned the job for the major league club that nearly every fan in the ballpark pays attention to."I am the captioner for the Pirates for the JumboTron," Sibley said.

He earned the job after he interned for the Pirates last summer through a program at the community college he attends.

It's a dream come true for a student who did not make great grades in high school but had a real talent he was unsure what to do with: typing very fast.

"I initially thought IT programming might be the way to go, but I found I didn't care for that. Then a teacher suggested court reporting. There weren't many options out there until I saw what CCAC had," Sibley said of Community College of Allegheny County, where he will be graduating early from in May.

Every year, more than 25,000 students enroll at that community college in the greater Pittsburgh area, picking one of more than 150 degree, certificate, diploma or transfer programs. On top of that are the thousands more who take workforce development courses at the school.

In a city that boasts six major universities within its city limits–University of Pittsburgh, Carnegie Mellon, Duquesne, Robert Morris, Chatham, Point Park, and Carlow–those are impressive numbers.

While enrollment at community colleges is down across the country, despite the dramatic cost savings of beginning there and either transferring or going straight into the workforce with an associate degree, the benefits schools such as Community College of Allegheny County have are immeasurable, not just for the students but also for the communities they serve.

A student pays $110 per credit here at the school, compared to around $800 at University of Pittsburgh or $1,406 at Harvard University. On average, student borrowers in higher learning institutions outside of community colleges owe $28,650, according to the nonprofit research and advocacy group Institute for College Access & Success.

The cost of higher education became a political football in America since 2016, when Sen. Bernie Sanders, I-Vt., made free college the core of his Democratic presidential primary campaign. His 2020 rivals have jumped on the bandwagon.

These schools help students such as Sibley find their niche, and they provide opportunity for students who weren't ready to put themselves or their parents in debt.

"I didn't really know what I wanted to do," Alex Lopez, 23, told me. "I was trying to figure out what I actually wanted to do. I'm like, 'Let me go give computer science a try.' Well, I gave it a try, and it really wasn't for me. I had a teacher tell me, 'Why don't you go into teaching?' I'm like, 'Sure, why not?' And I just set it off from there."

It was his parents who urged him to start his journey as a teacher at a community college.

"And I wanted to, to be honest. I didn't want to break their bank," he said of attending a larger university.

Lopez, who is half black and half Latino, decided teaching Spanish would be a natural fit for him. "Half of my family is fluent in Spanish," he said.

There's more. A community college often makes itself an integral part of its community. "We (are) situated inside of a community," Community College of Allegheny County President Dr. Quintin B. Bullock says, "and most of the time individuals who choose the community college as their point of access of higher education and workforce training, they are making a commitment to stay in the community."

Ninety-four percent of that university's students remain, live and work following graduation, Bullock says. "That affirms the importance of the community college."

While the majority of students in the other universities in the city leaves the region after graduation, a system of higher education that is affordable and retains the graduates locally, making the community younger, smarter and stronger, has to be better part of the national conversation as a solution for a variety of societal problems.

# After Mueller, Nobody Has Changed Their Views on Trump

*April 23, 2019*

Nothing has changed.

Just about no one has moved away from where they stood on Nov. 9, 2016, when they woke up trying to comprehend that Donald J. Trump had overcome the odds, the press and his own shortcomings to win that presidential election.

If you voted for him, you are still thrilled and optimistic about the future. I outlined in the book I co-authored with Brad Todd, "The Great Revolt," that the election was never quite about Trump. Many of his voters saw his flaws with eyes wide open and voted heavily out of concern for their community, not necessary for themselves.

Many who did not vote for Trump loathe him with the intensity of a white-hot poker prodding at their soul. Their hair is still on fire, and nothing in the world can extinguish it until he is out of the White House, preferably in handcuffs.

If you are a reporter who lives and works within the counties that surround Washington, D.C., New York, Chicago or Los Angeles, it's been a tough go. You don't work with anyone in your newsroom who would have voted for Trump. You don't socialize with anyone who voted for Trump. And you likely don't know anyone at your children's school who voted for Trump.

Many reporters, though not all, often view these voters monolithically rather than as the complex coalition they have formed, painting them with a broad brush. They see the Trump voters as foolish or fooled at best, and as bigoted, unintelligent and backward at worst.

Reporters marvel at these voters' unwillingness to give up on a struggling town and move to a larger city or region, never understanding that they often happily trade a higher salary or a career with bonuses in another city for staying in a community where they have deep roots.

Since the day after Trump won, reports on his win focused heavily on his loss of the popular vote. Then there were the overhyped stories about a Wisconsin recount. Then the story developed that he only won because of Russia and that he probably helped Russia "hack the election."

This simply reinforced Trump backers' support for the man. Haters will hate.

Which brings us back to this: Nothing has changed since Election Day 2016, because everything had changed for the C-suite influencers who control our culture, politics, entertainment, big tech and news consumption. They chose to ignore the signs–or, in their arrogance, they just missed what had been in plain sight for decades.

The fusion of conservatives and populists who make up the Trump coalition that placed Trump in the White House will continue long after whatever date the president leaves office. And despite the efforts of the press, and despite Trump's own actions, those in the Trump coalition are unlikely to change their mind, because the only alternative is an elite who paints them as a villainous segment of our society.

# Why Trump Is Bitter the Firefighters Endorsed Joe Biden

*April 30, 2019*

PITTSBURGH–Joe Biden's decision to kick off his presidential campaign in Western Pennsylvania Monday shows that he is not just in a battle for the soul of the country; he is in a battle for the soul of his party.

That battle begins and ends with long primary contests that many Democratic experts and officials believe will be decided exactly one year from now, on Pennsylvania's April 29 primary voting day.

"This nominating process certainly has all of the ingredients to go long, and the Democratic voters in this state hold the key to help defining our party as being the party of the working class," said Harold Schaitberger, the general president of the International Association of Fire Fighters, in an interview with The New York Post.

The IAFF, which represents more than 316,000 full-time firefighters and paramedics, announced its endorsement of Biden in Pittsburgh, something Schaitberger said is one of the earliest endorsements it's ever done, and one it did not give Hillary Clinton or Donald Trump in the 2016 election.

"That marked the first time we've ever not endorsed in a presidential election," he said.

Schaitberger bluntly admits Clinton just did not connect with labor, but Biden does.

"We're also responsible to make sure that, quite frankly, the nominee isn't a nominee that is gonna take the party off the left cliff," he said. "It seems that too many candidates have high-minded, aspirational ideals, but it's not a recipe for winning and succeeding. And it doesn't really reflect in many ways the heart and soul of workers, middle-class workers."

If you think the IAFF's influence in the Democratic primary process is not of significance, a moment in the 2004 election cycle is often overlooked, when former Vermont Gov. Howard Dean had captured the imagination and speculation among the press and pundits.

"As you know, Howard Dean was gonna be the nominee. It was that simple–at least, that is what everyone said, until all of a sudden, we snuck up and literally carried John through Iowa and through New Hampshire," Schaitberger said of John Kerry. "And then he was off and running in the rest of the world."

The decision to back Biden has already annoyed President Trump, who tweeted Monday, "The Dues Sucking firefighters leadership will always support Democrats, even though the membership wants me. Some things never change!"

Often, where the firefighters go, so do other union workers.

Harold McDonald, a Democratic committee man from Penn Hills, Pennsylvania, and retired council representative for the Carpenters Union, is convinced this race is going long: "This is truly the battle for the soul of our party. You have pundits and reporters on the national news saying our party is one thing, and then you have the rank and file voters here saying that's not what we are voting on at all."

McDonald, who is African American, said voters here worry about health care and education. "That is what is important to me as well," he said. "That is why I am supporting Biden already."

The same goes for 22-year-old Hannah O'Toole, who sang the national anthem at the Workers Memorial Day celebration in Pittsburgh ahead of Biden's visit along with her father, 60-year-old Marty O'Toole, who is the business manager for Plumbers Local 27.

"Joe Biden's been a big part of the way we think and want to go and he has always been a front runner for us here in Pennsylvania," said Marty O'Toole, who is personally supporting the former vice president.

Hannah O'Toole is also leaning toward Biden. "I've liked him since Obama," she said.

Darrin Kelly, president of the powerful local labor council here in Western Pennsylvania and a city firefighter, said the Party has drifted too far left. And this is the state where, not just in the general but mostly in the primary, that will be decided.

"Today is an important reminder of what is important to voters in Pennsylvania in a Democratic primary and we expect the Democratic Party to truly start listening to what our message is, stop polarizing us and start welcoming us back, we want FDR style politics," Kelly said. "If our strength is truly our diversity then the party has to start listening to the working class, they have to welcome us back and our voice will be heard in the primary in this state and that the message we want about job creation, health care and pension security is what will bring us out in a general."

# What's the Matter With Virginia?

*May 7, 2019*

LEXINGTON, Va.–Clare Perry considers herself a Democrat. Grayson Pearce is a Republican. She's from Richmond, and he's from Virginia Beach. Despite holding opposing political values, they both have the same question: What is the matter with Virginia?

In particular, what's wrong with its politics?

A few months ago, in a cascade of disgraces, both Gov. Ralph Northam and Attorney General Mark Herring admitted to having worn blackface. Then, Lt. Gov. Justin Fairfax was accused of sexual assault by two women.

Now the stories have seemingly disappeared from the front pages, or any pages, of the local news outlets.

For both Perry, 20, and Pearce, 19, the fact that all three controversies were left drifting in the wind is mind-boggling.

"Honestly, I'm stunned, and I'm stunned it went away so quickly," Perry explains. She's more bothered that Fairfax has skated.

For Pearce, there's a personal angle: He worked on the campaign of Northam's opponent, Ed Gillespie. But it also stings, in part, because it reflects poorly on the state he loves. He says: "It is heartbreaking. It sucks. There's nothing about it that's good. Especially not for Virginia."

Both readily agree that if Gillespie had faced the same accusations any of the three men in power did months ago, he would be long gone.

University of Virginia political analyst Kyle Kondik says Northam remains in office for a number of reasons: "For one thing, Fairfax is even more toxic than he is, and the accusations against the lieutenant governor help insulate the governor. But I also think the governor surveyed the political climate and determined that he was better off staying in office than resigning. Northam did, in fact, face a lot of pressure to resign, but he weathered it and decided not to step aside in spite of it."

Northam could not have been forced from office short of impeachment, which is a step the legislature decided not to take.

Though he largely won on anti-Trump anger, he is now less popular than the president in the state, according to the latest Wason Center for Public Policy poll.

Both parties seem to be struggling with leadership voids. The Republicans haven't won a statewide election since 2009, and the Democrats have three statewide officeholders who are all damaged to some degree.

"The environment for the fall campaign is in flux," said Kondik. "On one hand, the Democrats are banking on the white-hot, anti-Trump intensity that fueled them in 2017 and 2018. On the other, they are hamstrung to some degree by the weakness of Northam and Fairfax, and there also were some questions about Democratic turnout without a major statewide race on the ballot."

But there's still plenty at stake. Kondik said: "Democrats need to net two seats apiece in the state Senate and state House of Delegates to elect a unified Democratic state government, which would be the most liberal state government in Virginia history."

Those gains will be easier if a new court-drawn House of Delegates map that unwinds a Republican gerrymander is indeed in place for the fall. But it's not a certainty that they can or will capitalize.

You have to think of Virginia voting patterns as several different regions, and the political divide in the state as being primarily east versus west.

Kondick said: "The eastern part of the state contains its so-called 'Urban Crescent,' the major population centers of Northern Virginia, Greater Richmond, and Hampton Roads. The western part of the state is largely rural, with some smaller cities and college towns serving as blue pockets in what is otherwise a red sea."

The Urban Crescent has been becoming more Democratic, and the western part has been becoming more Republican. There are many more votes in the eastern part of the state than the western, so this trade-off has worked out well for Democrats.

Pearce said that as an aspiring political operative, he thinks the Republicans' focus in his home state is that geography outside of the cities, just before the rolling hills of the farmland.

"You have to focus on suburbia, especially women, white women. And really, there's a great opportunity, especially for where I'm from, Hampton Roads, a great opportunity to target minority voters. There are so many minority voters in Norfolk, Hampton, Newport News, Portsmouth, and they're all stuck in the same rut. Democrats are just counting on them because of the color of their skin. I think that there's a great opportunity for votes there, but if Republicans can't win suburbia, there's no path for them in Virginia," he said.

"Even with the scandals," he said.

# In Front of a Philadelphia Abortion Clinic, Democratic Lawmaker Shows Us the Darkness of the Cultural Divide

*May 14, 2019*

PHILADELPHIA–When Brian Sims first ran for state representative in 2012, he ran as a new pro-business voice. He was going to be a bridge builder, brimming with common-sense ideas on pocketbook issues.

He never met that promise.

Instead, he became many other things: an outdoor adventurer who climbed Mt. Kilimanjaro; a partisan attack dog who accused fellow state Rep. Martina White of saying she wanted to deport all immigrants, something his staff had to admit she never said; and a celebrity activist whose lucrative, nationwide speaking circuit earned him an ethics investigation.

He also became the guy who tweeted a photo of himself wearing a suit and a smirk and raising his middle finger to Vice President Mike Pence.

Sims captioned the photo saying: "(L)et me be the first to officially welcome you to the City of Brotherly Love and my District! We're a City of soaring diversity. We believe in the power of all people. Black, Brown, Queer, Trans, Atheist, & Immigrant. So ... get bent, then get out!"

Last week, Sims decided to film his own harassment of a woman outside an abortion clinic here in Philadelphia, calling her an "old white lady" and her beliefs "grotesque" to her face and to the camera. The clear plan was to incite his audience against this peaceful protester, whom he saw as clearly bigoted and evil.

For Twitter observers, the whole act opened the window into a dark, dark place in American culture, a gaping divide none of us quite know how to navigate.

And while Sims' harassment was, on the one hand, shocking, it was expected. A politician abusing his power thusly to crush religious conservatives is exactly what so many of us have been bracing for.

This was no outburst in the heat of a debate. He wasn't reacting to a stressful situation. It also wasn't a talk-show appearance that went sour, nor was it a barroom brawl. He wasn't caught off guard at his home or his office or a campaign event.

This was an emboldened, out-of-touch, arrogant elected official who woke up one day last week and made a conscious decision to go to Planned Parenthood for the express purpose of fighting and badgering.

And he chose a woman standing by herself. And he didn't start a dialogue. He didn't introduce himself. He badgered her. Repeatedly. Relentlessly. Angrily. He badgered an enemy he himself described as an old lady.

Then he badgered women younger than he, asking his Twitter following to identify them and expose them for the crime of being anti-abortion.

Sims not only chose to do this; he did this with malice aforethought.

And how do we know that? Because he himself filmed it. This wasn't caught on film by an anti-abortion activist or passerby. Sims filmed it all on purpose. Then, having done these things, having behaved this way and presumably, viewed this film, he released it with great fanfare, regaled himself for what he had done and asked people to send money to, in essence, support their shared views, values and cause.

We must reflect on this. This is the extreme left acting out in public in exactly the manner they ascribe to conservatives:

confrontational, intimidating, with police tactics, berating women, threatening the First Amendment.

This stunning behavior–premeditated, confrontational, abusive of the power of office, targeted toward women, contrived to gain political benefit–occurred and has not been criticized by anyone on the left. No elected Democrat has come out and condemned Sims publicly.

Think about that.

This is not about anti-abortion and pro-abortion. This is about behavior that is so out of step, so out of line, so shocking to most of America but is allowed to occur without a word of disapproval from half the country.

# Real America Sits at One End of the Potomac–and at the Other

*May 21, 2019*

    GORMANIA, W.Va.–Life here along the North Branch of the Potomac River is very different than life 162 miles downriver.

There is raw natural beauty that takes your breath away. Under your feet flows the Potomac, above you the Allegheny Plateau, and the ascent toward Mt. Storm beckons with forests filled with red spruce, balsam fir and mountain ash.

    Hawks and eagles float above you. Snakes, deer, squirrels and bears walk or slither past you.

    Then there's the tragic beauty in town. Along U.S. Route 50, buildings that once held banks and stores and homes stand as memorials of a different time–abandoned by circumstance, failure or loss, they hold their place like stone sentinels, erosion licking at their facades.

    No one who lives here can remember things being any different.

    The Gormania Gas & Go does business amid this decay. Its breakfast sandwich is served fresh, hot, tasty and with plenty of hospitality–the kind of thing you find in gas stations across the Midwest and South, where people come not just for fuel but also to connect and chat about anything that comes to mind.

    The churches left long ago. The Presbyterian church shuttered in 1994. The Methodist one followed in 2003, both due to loss in attendance. There is still one coal mine left in operation, but the heyday of coal here was decades ago.

When Chandra Delaney and her family got here in 1971, the place was already collapsed. "The center of town has sort of always looked like that," she says.

Delaney's family stayed and thrived. When she grew up and married, she stayed, too, and also thrived. Her grown daughters have also stayed and thrived: One is a teacher, the other a hygienist. As we chat, her granddaughter's school bus pulls up to drop her off at the stores she runs along U.S. 50 heading toward Mt. Storm.

"You get tied to a place," she says. "It becomes part of you, and you become part of it."

Delaney is working at Sit a Spell, the general store she operates along the ridge of the mountain. "The name came from something my dad used to always say, and meant a lot to me about community and storytelling and just getting together," she says.

For five years, she operated it as the Sit a Spell diner. She changed it to a general store for a couple of reasons: People needed groceries, health products, beauty products, cleaning supplies and school supplies; also, the business of running a diner can wear on a person.

Her husband, John, is a union electrician who drives 70 miles back and forth from his job at the other end of the state. He says: "You do what you have to do. No need to complain about it. We made the decision to stay put, and once you make a choice it seems silly to spend the rest of your time complaining about the choice you made."

At the other end of the Potomac River, Washington, D.C., offers a different kind of beauty. It's a city built partly on a swamp but mostly on old tobacco fields. The city entrances you with her glistening monuments, stately museums, handsome homes and beautiful parks. She also overwhelms you with her overabundance of power and affluence.

Here only the few stay put, despite all the growth reflected in the never-ending construction of new condos, townhouses and apartment buildings.

Both of these places along the Potomac tell the story of America. Neither of them is the "real" story. They're both just part of the whole story–something we all forget from time to time.

In D.C., Martin Luther King gave his famous "I Have a Dream" speech. He understood the importance of place and culture when he said, "Let freedom ring from the heightening Alleghenies of Pennsylvania!"

King knew exactly what "staying put" meant when he wrote that. And he knew exactly why it was important to say: Division wasn't his game. He knew, as a country and for his cause, that drawing those fabrics of place together was critical.

I asked Delaney what she thinks is the biggest difference between her end of the Potomac and the Washington end.

"Pretty much the cost of living," she said. "Other than that, aren't we all in this together?"

# Coming Home

*May 28, 2019*

No matter where you lived in America on the morning of Sept. 11, 2001, the story often begins with a sapphire sky filled with airy, white clouds that perfectly contrasted against the expansive blue, a picture-perfect backdrop shattered by the deadliest attack on American soil in the country's history.

Nineteen men trained by al Qaida boarded four passenger aircrafts that morning, seeking to carry out a devastating coordinated attack aimed at symbols of American freedom: the World Trade Center, the Capitol and the Pentagon. Three hit their target. Flight 93, the plane targeting the Capitol, crashed in an isolated field in Somerset County, Pennsylvania, thanks to brave passengers who wrested control of the plane from the hijackers. Almost 3,000 people lost their lives that day, 400 of whom were New York City's first responders.

Taylor Cleveland and Victor Lewis are two people whose lives were changed by the terror attacks. They were separated by geography, age and life experience, but for them, 9/11 proved to be a common call of duty to serve their country. The Washington Examiner spoke with them about their service.

Ohioan Taylor Cleveland grew up surrounded by soldiers.

He says: "Even my priest growing up was a chaplain in World War II. I mean, everybody around here served. It's just expected that's what you're going to do."

Unfortunately, he couldn't follow in the footsteps of others. He had been a local high school football star and had wrecked his knee during a game, so the Marine Corps turned him down. Instead, Cleveland turned to community service, earned a degree in criminal justice and then worked as an emergency medical technician, a firefighter and then a beat cop before joining the department SWAT team.

But he knew he had to do something more after the 9/11 attacks.

He says: "My grandfather joined the Navy the day after Pearl Harbor in 1941. And I just knew after that there was no way they would keep me out of this war that was coming. There was no way that people were going to go fight a war for me and that they were going to put their lives on the line for me. I could never live with myself as a man if I didn't go and let somebody else go fight my battles for me."

He signed up to join the Marine Reserves but had concerns about his knee injury.

"I figured that because I had the knee problem still, they'd still turn me down," he recalls. "Well, they enlisted me before the medical portion, and they called the house and left a message on the machine that said, 'Good news, you're approved.'"

Lewis and Cleveland met in Buffalo, New York, in 2003. Cleveland is 3rd Battalion, 25th Marines. Lewis, a Navy hospital corpsman, was attached to the Marine unit. The two became like brothers immediately.

They deployed to Iraq in 2005. Cleveland admits he had a hard time adjusting at first: "I was friends with a fellow reservist by the name of Jeff Wiener who had joined the Marines right out of high school. Wiener's got this book, and it's got a picture and a story of every person that was killed in 9/11, and I'm like, 'What are you doing, bro?' He smiles at me, and he's like, 'Man, I just read this whole book. I can tell you what, I read every single person that was in here that died on 9/11. I know why I'm here.'"

Twenty minutes after that conversation, Wiener was fatally shot in the head. Cleveland recalls, "That's the last conversation I had with him. Having him say, 'Man, I know why I'm here,' is the best gift I've been given."

Lewis says he never got shot in Iraq. No mortar. No shrapnel.

Cleveland practically spits out his beer as he says, "Dude, you were hit by a rocket!"

Lewis is sheepish and uncomfortable telling the story. Deployed south of Haditha, just outside Haqlaniyah, the engagement turned deadly as a guy coming straight at Lewis fired off a rocket-propelled grenade.

He explains: "The blast throws me toward the river. Trying to shake it off, I grab my weapon. I'm trying to fire back. I'm crawling toward the river. I go to stand up and fall back down. Like, 'What the f---?' My leg's all mangled."

He was medevaced to Al Asad Air Base and then took a Black Hawk to Basra. From there, he was transported to Ramstein, Germany, and finally, Bethesda, Maryland. He wanted a little Motrin and to go back to "his men," but they told him he was going home.

"I felt like I failed them, you know? Because nobody could take care of my men like me," Lewis says. "They're my boys. We hung out. We partied. We kicked it. We shared everything. I wanted to go back."

That's the hardest part of returning to civilian life. "I think about it all the time," he says. "But you know ... you can replay it as many times as you like in your mind. The result's the same."

Lewis is blunt about his routine after leaving the military: "hanging out, drinking and chasing women."

He finally went back to work at the fire department, but even working triple shifts couldn't fill the void left by having to do something other than what he saw as his purpose in life.

He sought help from the Department of Veterans Affairs and got lost in the system. Lewis says, "I started snapping at people and flipping out over nothing, but that's not me. I was looking for help."

It all came to a head one evening outside a bar when he was approached by two men and a woman looking for trouble. They pummeled Lewis pretty badly; he fought back with a knife.

"People got hurt," is all he says. The price? Thirty months in prison.

But he turned his life around. He gets treatment for his post-traumatic stress disorder, has a job he loves at a contracting company and takes care of his twin boys. He talks to Cleveland at least twice a week and is working toward his degree in electrical engineering.

Lewis earned a Bronze Star, and Cleveland a Purple Heart. The lesson they want people to remember is simple: American freedom is paid for a thousand different ways.

# It Can Take a Foreigner to Teach Us the American Dream

*June 4, 2019*

NORTH VERSAILLES, Penn.–Starr DeJesus admits she learned a lot about both the generosity of the American people and her own potential from an immigrant who spoke to her civics class.

"I didn't know it was just an America thing to tip servers," the high school senior and part-time Denny's server said. "We rarely emphasize the good things about our culture. The only things you ever hear about on social media are complaints or criticisms."

DeJesus said she also didn't consider how much it is within her own power to earn more money. "You gotta push," she said. "Some people you really have to impress and wow to get that tip. If you do the bare minimum, they're not going to care and they're going to disregard you. But, me personally, I try my best every day. That's why I have a lot of regulars, and I'm able to earn so much money being this young. But it is a lesson I will take with me to college and eventually my career."

The larger lesson she and 100 or so other high school students here at East Allegheny High School learned was something they sheepishly admitted afterward that they had taken for granted: how lucky they are to be born in America.

Nick Adams, the immigrant from Australia who spoke to the students, appreciates this in a way a native may never truly understand.

When Adams was a boy, an American doctor, who happened to be interning in Australia, successfully diagnosed the rare cancer he had. Adams points to that moment as evidence of American exceptionalism.

He has since dedicated his life to reminding young people through his nonprofit, the Foundation for Liberty & American Greatness, of all the aspects that make this country truly unique. On this blustery spring day, he was in the Mon Valley discussing with these students why they should remember America's greatness.

The students were riveted by Adams' perspective. His questions engaged them and challenged them on the benefits of their citizenship, which he equates to winning the lottery.

"OK, so in my hand I have a coin," he says. "I want to ask you, there are three things inscribed on every coin in U.S. currency and printed on every dollar bill of every denomination in American currency. Who can tell me what those three things are?"

The students provide the answers: "In God we trust," "e pluribus unum" and "liberty."

"I like to call it the American trinity," Adams says. "Some of you might have heard the holy Trinity. I like to call it the American trinity. Those three things make America a unique place. Some countries have one of those things. Some countries have two of those things. But no other country in the world has the unique blend of each of those three different things. Liberty, e pluribus unum, and in God we trust."

East Allegheny High School is an ordinary high school campus located in a tidy middle-class neighborhood that has seen better days economically. It is nonetheless surrounded by modest homes whose owners clearly take great pride in their appearance.

It is a town that has not succumbed to the hollowed-out blight common among river towns in the Rust Belt. But the shrinking population has led to a smaller school district: There are 724 students seventh through 12th grade. The student body is 57% white and 30% black.

Fifty-seven percent of the 2018 graduates went to a four-year college. Thirty-eight percent went to community college. Three percent went to a trade school. And 1% joined the Army.

Marissa Riggs, a senior from the nearby borough of Wilmerding, was told by her honors history teacher to come to the presentation. "Honestly I am glad it was compulsory," she said. "I really learned a lot."

"I thought Mr. Adams was really inspiring. He reminded us powerful things we sometimes take for granted, such as we are a government of the people, not a people of the government," she said, adding, "I think we're a little bit too spoiled and entitled sometimes in our thinking."

Perhaps learning, like everything else in our daily lives, is too laced with politics, and simply delivering the details to students in a compelling way can help make understanding all of history, good and bad, a lot more meaningful.

# Finding America at a Back-Roads Gas Station

*June 11, 2019*

DICKERSON, Md.–Everything happens for a reason.

At least that's what people tell you when your plans go south.

Driving from Pittsburgh to Washington, D.C., recently, I did as I nearly always do: I clicked the "avoid highways" option on Google Maps and chose a route I'd never taken before.

You'd be amazed by the number of different routes you can take between western Pennsylvania and our nation's capital. This one took me through the heights of the Laurel Mountains toward the original Lincoln Highway, where I went through the delightful town of Mercersburg and then due south toward U.S. 40, the original National Pike. Eventually, I slowly snaked along the Maryland side of the Potomac River southeast toward D.C.

This way of traveling lets you see, even if only fleetingly, the towns, unincorporated villages and cities that sometimes connect on one single U.S. route. On these roads, you see the differences in prosperity, density and decay that make up America.

As I approached a bend in the road that passes under an ancient stone train bridge along Maryland Route 28, it happened. The flat-tire warning signals began flashing across my dashboard. I didn't have a choice. I had to try to navigate past the sharp curve, through the narrow underpass, and pray there was somewhere flat to pull over on the other side.

I am fairly sure I completed a world-record 30-second recital of the rosary in my head as I made it around the bend. Then I took in the damage. My tire was shredded.

The Dickerson Market looks like the hundreds of general stores I see every time I hit the back roads. It has a post office attached to it, not to mention no-name self-service gasoline pumps in the front and a sign boasting "famous fried chicken."

On that day, it was my oasis.

To those passing through, these general stores are just gas stations. But to people who live here or come to the area regularly for the hiking, biking and fishing, places like Dickerson Market are the center of the community. It's where they can get an amazing breakfast sandwich hot off the grill or donate to Toys for Tots. It's where they can buy a birthday card, a winter hat or groceries, or where they can sit for a spell at a handful of tables and chairs.

It is where conversations spring up among strangers, with the grace and charity you won't find on social media or cable news.

I certainly found that grace and charity in the hours I waited there for AAA. I also found a microcosm of America in the veritable parade of strangers who helped and offered to help.

A white couple with more tattoos than I could possibly count, a group of young Hispanic men and an African American couple all offered different forms of assistance for my obvious distress.

Michelle Ennis isn't surprised by the hospitality shown by the patrons of her store. "I see that type of kindness from our regulars in little things every day," she says. "This place is a piece of history as well as a reflection of our community. We may change, because we have to change with moderation and things like that. But you still have down-to-the-basics, pleasant people. ... You miss that in the cities. I've been in cities, and you can hardly get someone to say hello to you or look you in the eye."

Ennis owns the store with her father, Robert Fowler, who bought it 22 years ago. He was a regular, and the former owners wanted someone who cared about the community to carry on the tradition they began in 1948. Michelle Ennis' kids work behind the counter, and her husband helps when things break down. "It is a real family operation," she says.

More than 1,000 pieces of their fried chicken leave the unassuming general store while I wait for my tow.

To anyone passing by, this just looks like a gas station. To anyone who takes the time to step inside, they will find themselves in a wonderland.

It is Memorial Day weekend, and no tire stores are open to repair my car. AAA tells me the dispatch will tow my car home to Pittsburgh, and I'll get to ride along. The anxiety that starts to overwhelm me as I wonder how I am going to interact with a stranger for 5 1/2 hours in the small space of a tow truck quickly evaporates minutes after Krasimir Georgiev shows up to take me and my bruised Jeep home.

An immigrant from Bulgaria, Georgiev's story makes the time fly. He arrived from Germantown with little money and an uncertain future. Now he's a small-business man who owns two tow trucks and employs several people.

Grace always finds a way to show up just in time. I've written that before, and I say it often. Even though I know it will come, it's always surprising where you find it. Sometimes it's on a back road in Maryland that you thought you were taking for no good reason. But it turns out there was a reason.

# What Happens When Joe Stops Being Joe?

*June 18, 2019*

FACTORYVILLE, Pa.–Joe Biden has always gotten away with being Joe Biden.

This was true when he was President Barack Obama's vice president, and it was true for his decades in the Senate.

"That's just Joe being Joe," reporters, politicians and commentators would say with a chuckle whenever Biden said something outrageous or awkward, or when he behaved bizarrely. "Classic Biden!"

But what happens if Joe stops being Joe?

What if he starts being no different from his 20-plus competitors?

One month after Biden rolled out a near-perfect presidential announcement, bookending his tour in his home state of Pennsylvania, Biden started to become a little less Joe. His opponents, special interest groups and his own campaign staff leaned him on the question of abortion subsidies, and so he flipped, abandoning his longtime support for the Hyde Amendment.

Keep in mind that pressure came from people who, for the most part, do not live in proximity to the very voters who will likely decide a presidential election, who instead live in the same super ZIP codes that surround Washington and New York City. Everyone they know supports federal subsidies for abortion. That taxpayer dollars for abortion would upset some Democrats or independents is unthinkable to this crowd.

This same crowd that advised Hillary Clinton persuaded Biden. And that is when Joe stopped being Joe.

"This kind of abrupt change in policy stances flies in the face of Biden's strengths," said Jeff Brauer, political science professor at Keystone College here in Factoryville, "particularly in a general election."

David Axelrod, the chief strategist for the 2008 and 2012 Obama-Biden presidential campaigns, tweeted in response to Biden's flip: "The @JoeBiden rollout was close to flawless. His handling of this Hyde Amendment issue was a mess. Changes of position over a long career are justifiable but should be thoughtfully planned. This was an awkward flip-flop-flip."

The Hyde Amendment has long been part of the pragmatic compromise on the emotionally charged issue of abortion, explained Brauer. "While Americans are generally OK with early-term abortions as an option," he said, "they generally don't believe tax dollars should be paying for them, especially since so many Americans are morally opposed to abortions."

Biden has for decades cautiously straddled the line on this issue despite his party's much more liberal stances on it. It was a position that has helped to solidify his image as practical and respectful on difficult issues.

Brauer warns that Biden's newfound support for taxpayer-funded abortions will jeopardize his appeal to pragmatic Midwest voters who went for Trump in 2016.

"While this flip may assist him in maintaining support from the Democratic base, it is likely to dissuade the independents and moderates needed to win the general election over Trump," he said.

"What Biden needs to do is appeal to voters in the middle and even the Right," Brauer argues. "This move isn't going to help in that. Moving hard left in the primary could prove to be fatal for the general."

"Biden has also succumbed to far-left pressures on the environment by rolling out a policy plan that is far more liberal than expected," said Brauer.

Trump's victory in 2016 was primarily due to his support in the Midwestern Rust Belt states, whose voters had been hit hard economically as jobs moved elsewhere. With a recent boom fueled by natural gas, some of these areas are bouncing back.

Brauer said: "These voters will see stronger environmental regulations as a major threat to continued financial success. While Biden has been effective in the past in reaching blue-collar workers, prospective new regulations will be a game changer for their support if they feel Biden's environmental policies are going to hit them in their pocketbooks."

Brauer said Biden truly needs to rethink short-term gains in the primary, which could cost him his long-term strengths in the general. "These concessions to the Left will lead to new questions concerning his stances on other issues," he said. "In turn, that could end up pushing him even further to the left, perhaps to the point where he will no longer be seen as just Joe."

In an era when voters were able to look at Trump and understand exactly what sort of man he was yet vote for him anyway, a less-than-genuine Biden hardly seems to be in demand. Voters want you to be who you are, rather than a creation of staffers, special interest groups and Washingtonians.

Just ask Clinton.

# Richard Trumka and Big Labor Try to Come Home

*June 25, 2019*

PITTSBURGH–Richard Trumka needed to come home.

Walking into the union hall at the Pittsburgh Federation of Teachers building along the Monongahela River, the AFL-CIO president shed the twisted expression on his face as he shook hands with his rank-and-file organizers. With the older union hands, there were no handshakes but instead familiar hugs.

Trumka, the son and son-in-law of coal miners, grew up in this region, working the coal mines himself, in the hollers of the mountains before heading off to college.

He rose up the ranks of the United Mine Workers of America union during the bloody strikes in the 1980s and eventually became the head of the 12.5 million-member AFL-CIO, the nation's largest labor union.

His passionate speech on race and labor in support of Barack Obama in 2008 is legend around these parts.

Trumka seems to recognize the men and women in the room here are the men and women who were ignored in the last presidential election. Hillary Clinton ignored them, not because she didn't want their vote but because she took it for granted. Clinton's campaign even persuaded union leadership that microtargeting voters on gender issues was more important than peer-to-peer communication among union families on the issues of jobs and opportunities.

Clearly, it wasn't. The blue wall of Pennsylvania, Ohio, Michigan and Wisconsin crumbled in 2016. Exit polls showed Clinton did win union households, but her shortfall among these households, compared with Obama's numbers, was her downfall in Michigan, at least.

Democrats had lost sight of what mattered to working people, and they had made the union bosses forget as well.

During the 2016 election, labor leaders got caught in the middle of several transitions, explained Paul Sracic, a political science professor at Youngstown State University: "For years they walked lockstep with the Democratic Party. This made sense, because most Republicans were tone-deaf to the concerns of labor, and the Democratic Party still had enough social conservatives in it to allow union members, many of whom were very socially conservative, to not feel out of place."

As the Democrats rapidly moved to the left on social issues and embraced identity politics, rank-and-file union members began to feel alienated from their own party. Economic interests, including trade, kept many of them in the party, but they were leaving even before Donald Trump.

When Trump went after trade, however, they got the push that they needed to join Trump's party, explained Sracic. "Leadership, however, was busy in Washington D.C. and had longstanding relationships with Democratic politicians," he said. "Hanging out with Republicans seemed unnatural, and in fairness, most of the Republicans in Congress, especially the Senate, wouldn't have much to talk about with someone like Richard Trumka."

In a way, though, the union leaders got co-opted and just went along with the leftward shift on social issues.

And as the Democratic Party became more coastal, its core voters became increasingly internationalist, including on trade.

Obama papered over these differences, running on anti-trade rhetoric to please people like Trumka and then governing as a free trader.

"The rank-and-file union members lost faith in the Democrats, and now leaders like Trumka are in a difficult position," Sracic said.

Trumka kicked off a three-day tour, beginning in Pittsburgh Monday and followed with stops in Youngstown, Akron, Cleveland and Toledo in Ohio, as well as Detroit, in the following days. Why? To reconnect with "the people." He wanted to hear what workers think about the new United States-Mexico-Canada Agreement, a trade agreement to replace the hated NAFTA.

"This tour is the people purpose. One it is to inform our members of the state of the negotiations we're at with the trade agreement. And two, it's to hear from them–get some instructions back from them," he said.

Darrin Kelly, president of the Allegheny County Labor Council, said the AFL-CIO affiliate was pleased by Trumka's visit. "It is important that we are heard. And we want everybody to know that the Rust Belt still has a strong voice in organized labor," he said.

Dave Green was at Trumka's roundtable visit in Youngstown. Green is the president of UAW Local 1112 and one of the final seven UAW workers to turn out the lights at the now shuttered General Motors Lordstown Assembly Plant. He does not think labor failed the workers in his area in the last election. "I think the Democratic Party failed labor," he said. "They did not talk about jobs, or opportunity, or the dignity of work."

"And that's why Trump won in my hometown, because that's all he wanted to talk about: jobs and opportunity," said Green, who himself did not vote for Trump.

It's unclear who will earn labor's support in 2020, but it's crystal clear to Trumka what union leadership has to do, and he tells me his plan before he approaches the podium: "Listen."

# 'Real America' Inside the Beltway

*July 2, 2019*

WASHINGTON–It is often said our nation's capital is filled with wealthy college-educated elites operating in a company town where everything is transactional. They are a clubby set of folks who can "fail up" in their profession and rarely interact meaningfully with anyone who isn't part of their peerage. They have lost touch with whomever they used to be wherever they used to come from.

Certainly, on the surface, things here look that way. But that is only the veneer.

Washington also serves as a destination point for Americans from across the country who often save up all year to bring their families to experience all of the history that has gone into forming this country. They visit both large and small museums; the U.S. Capitol; and the memorials honoring Thomas Jefferson, Abraham Lincoln and the brave men and women who fought in World War II, the Korean War and Vietnam.

At the Lincoln Memorial one recent day, thousands of parents, children and grandparents climbed the 87 marble steps from the reflecting pool to the feet of the 16th president. Dozens of languages filled the air as young entrepreneurs swiftly dodged park rangers to sell ice-cold water from makeshift carts. "Dollar water! Dollar water!" chants formed crowds around the cheerful young capitalists.

With the Washington Monument in the distance, a group of sorority sisters dressed to the nines who said they graduated from

Howard University together years ago laughed at their follies as they tried to orchestrate a selfie.

Just 300 yards northwest of the tourism bustle, a different sojourner was found at "the wall." Hundreds walked silently and respectfully past the chronological list of over 58,000 men and women who gave their lives in service to this country in Vietnam.

One man, his cap noting his service, stood with his hand touching a name, weeping quietly. His skin bronze, his dark hair was streaked with white and pulled back in a ponytail. He was briefly inconsolable. His wife began singing a chant, the chords anguished. Strangers one by one gently patted his back as they passed by.

His wife said, "It is a blessings chant ... for healing."

Two blocks away, a different anguish was visible in an encampment of homeless people on E Street, within eyesight of the State Department and the leafy campus of George Washington University. People who have grown used to this anguish hurry past.

City officials insist their family homeless problem has abated. There is irony to the rows of tents filled with people unable to make some sort of go of it in a city surrounded by six of the 10 richest U.S. counties.

Washington is just as complex as the small towns in Middle America that are often cast as homogeneous stretches of uneducated, immobile, resentful bigots.

In the past few months, I have driven through the back roads of Maryland, Virginia, West Virginia, North Carolina, South Carolina, Indiana, Ohio, Pennsylvania, Michigan and probably some other states I am forgetting. My experiences are always the same: People are nice, helpful, giving, imperfect, hardworking, deeply proud of where they come from and profoundly aspirational, no matter what trials they are struggling with.

But here's the irony: As much as Beltway insiders are told they need to get out of D.C. and see the real America, they could see the real America in their backyard if they were to open their eyes.

We often miss what is right in front of us, no matter where we live. A several-mile walk through Washington reminded me that it truly does represent all of the aspirations, weaknesses and failures you can see and experience anywhere in this country.

## In North Carolina Special, National Questions Intrude on Local Issues

*July 9, 2019*

WADESBORO, North Carolina–By the end of the summer, towns such as this will be flooded with national reporters covering the special election for the 9th Congressional District.

In normal times, reporters would ask voters how they think Republican Dan Bishop or Democrat Dan McCready would represent their local concerns in Washington. But these are not normal times.

Instead, the questions will mostly be about Donald Trump, and about Kamala Harris or Joe Biden or Pete Buttigieg.

The very existence of this race is abnormal, in fact. Voters in this district, which reaches from here to central Charlotte, have to come back for a do-over because of voter fraud in the November 2018 election.

The 2018 Republican nominee, Mark Harris, the center of the tainted votes, has dropped out of the do-over race, citing health issues. Instead Bishop, a state senator, will face McCready, the businessman who lost to Harris in that race.

Bob Orr, a former justice on the state Supreme Court, is one of those voters whose visceral distaste for Trump has incensed him so much that he abandoned his Republican roots to support McCready over Bishop, a man he admits he knows.

"I've always had a cordial relationship with Dan," Orr said. "Dan Bishop's an ideologue. He is a very, very conservative ideologue and if elected will go to Congress and just fall in line with whatever the Trump crowd tells him they need to do."

Orr was the state chairman of John Kasich's campaign in 2016 and a delegate to the Republican convention–until he walked out in protest of Trump.

"I'm adamantly opposed to the NRA using the Second Amendment as a fundraising tool," he said, but he admits there is a slight hypocrisy because the Democrats do the same thing in reverse.

"A plague and pox on both houses," he answers.

He is an example of the suburban moderate Republican who fled the Party and handed Democrats the House in 2018.

Bishop understands the risks of the race becoming too nationalized in the closing weeks this summer because of voters such as Orr who let their distaste for the president veer them away from their conservative roots.

He said: "I run into that some. Not as much as you might think. I was the only Republican to be reelected in November of 2018 in Mecklenburg County, where the wins were running in the other direction and there was some sentiment running against the President. I think that sentiment has attenuated." Many of the suburban voters in his home base of Charlotte have overcome their reservations about the president, Bishop says, "and have come to see him as an essential fighter."

Bishop also keenly understands that a realignment has happened in his party and he needs to adapt if he's going to be a good representative. His focus, he says, is on affordable health care, school choice and lifting up the economics in the rural areas.

"In Charlotte, where I'm from, it had been an up-and-coming, booming urban center," he said. "There's tremendous economic opportunities there. It has its own challenges, but bridging that gap and extending those opportunities to the more rural areas of North Carolina are absolutely critical."

And that begins, he says, with health care: "There are a lot of folks who have hospitals that have closed or are in danger of closing at all points. The national health care policy that we've seen towards a bigger government-dominated health care space, insurance that may be provided through ACA (Affordable Care Act) but with deductibles that they can't afford to use it."

"It is something that is not serving people's needs," he said. "They need a highly competitive health care space that will result in transparency, so that consumers are brought into the decision making and can over time help bring down costs, and yet make health care access better. That's critical."

McCready, for his part, isn't ceding 1 inch of his chances or the issue of health care to Bishop. The former Marines captain who served in Iraq sees Obamacare as essential.

He said: "We need to stick to the ACA. I would say the problem is not coming up with common-sense reform to lower health care costs, while maintaining coverage. The problem is that we don't have the people in Washington who will sit down and work together to do it."

Like the lesser-known new House moderates who won in swing suburban districts across the country last year but often exist in the shadow of Rep. Alexandria Ocasio-Cortez, McCready would like join the bipartisan House "problem-solvers" caucus.

He says: "The thing that I found with North Carolina is that you have the vast majority of people want to put country over political party. Whether you're a Republican or an independent, or you're a Democrat."

Both men are bracing for the race to go national in the final stretch and are trying to keep the focus on issues rather than personalities.

## Party, Personality, a Big Name and a Primary in Western Michigan

*July 16, 2019*

GRAND RAPIDS, Michigan–Peter Meijer's decision to run for Congress in Western Michigan was a surprise to no one who knows the 31-year-old Grand Rapids native.

He is the great-grandson of Hendrik Meijer, who opened a tiny thrift store attached to his barbershop during the Great Depression, which has since grown into a chain of groceries, department stores and gas stations across the Midwest. But Peter has always had his own idea of where his life is headed.

Instead of choosing a safe path within the family business, Meijer (rhymes with "dryer") pursued and earned an appointment to West Point, only to leave after his first year and enlist in the Army Reserves.

"I like to say that going there was the best decision I ever made and leaving was the hardest," he said of his resolution. "I loved the Army. I loved the military. But I really wanted to have the experience of being enlisted. But feeling like everything that I have I'm truly earning it ... that nothing is given to me because of my rank or because of any other factors but that at every step of the way, I could look back and know that what I am is because of what I've done and only that."

Meijer said he was in Iraq in 2010 and 2011 with his Army Reserve unit and then went to Afghanistan with an NGO two years later.

Since then, Meijer has been involved in a series of veteran advocacy groups including Team Rubicon and has jumped on an advisory board of a political action committee called With Honor that focuses on electing veterans.

Meijer knows well the incumbent, Justin Amash, and has supported him in the past. Amash's behavior convinced him to run. Specifically, Meijer says he felt compelled to run once Amash turned his focus to complaining about Donald Trump and took his focus off serving the district.

"One of the things that people in West Michigan really prize is just the sense of working together," he said. "This is not a fussy, dramatic part of the world. The community leaders spend a lot of time really supporting the community."

Grandstanding about feelings doesn't fit in.

He said: "I feel obligated to continue to find a way to contribute to my country. I'm not so arrogant as to think that running for Congress is a valiant exercise in self-sacrifice, but I feel like I've had some very formative and strong experiences, and that having more of those experiences in Congress is going to help."

Meijer is one of five candidates running for the GOP nomination that is now open after Amash announced he would run as an independent. Three Democrats have also declared including Nick Colvin, a former Obama staffer.

Amash, who has also teased the idea of a run against Trump for president, faces a series of challenges in his own state. For years, Michigan has had straight-ticket voting: Press one button and you vote for every Republican or every Democrat or every Libertarian or whatever you want.

In 2018, Michigan didn't have straight-ticket voting; the Republican legislature and former Republican governor had taken it off. Ballot Proposal 3, which passed overwhelmingly in the state in 2018, put straight-ticket voting back into the state constitution.

In short, the voters themselves chose to empower a two-party system. That makes winning as an independent very hard.

Meijer said bluntly: "I haven't lost faith in the Republican Party. I think we can be the party of the future. We can represent and offer better solutions to the problems facing the United States that are founded on conservative principles of limited government, economic freedom and individual liberty."

He added: "I think in the political process today we spend way too much time on the right dismissing problems or mocking Democrats when they offer a solution instead of offering solutions of our own. And that's something that I really think we need to do if we're going to especially appeal to younger generations."

# Lara Trump Tries to Fix Her Party's Woman Problem

*July 23, 2019*

KING OF PRUSSIA, Pa.–Last week, one month before she was set to give birth to her second child, Lara Trump came here to kick off the 2020 Women for Trump coalition, planting a flag, or at least an olive branch, in some of the least Trump-friendly terrain in the Keystone State: suburban Philadelphia.

Poised, witty and sharply on message, President Trump's daughter-in-law is a natural in a position she says is far removed from her modest upbringing. "I grew up in a middle-class family in North Carolina, and I couldn't have ever imagined that I would be a part of anything like this," she told me.

Her job is both simple and complicated: keeping the old female voters and persuading the new ones for her father-in-law, who, to be frank, has a woman problem. The foundation of his base has been and continues to be men, explained Jeff Brauer, political science professor at Keystone College. "Particularly married men, who voted for Trump nearly 20 points higher than Clinton in 2016," he said. "To be accurate though, it is not just a Trump problem. Single women, who make up almost half of the women in the country, tend to be strongly Democratic. In 2016, Clinton won unmarried women by almost 30 points."

Single men also went to Hillary Clinton but by a tiny 2-point margin.

"So the real key is married women. They will decide the next presidency," said Brauer.

Lara Trump says her biggest challenge isn't retaining the women who voted for her father-in-law in 2016; instead, it's winning the votes of women who didn't vote for him but now find they like his policies while disliking his comportment.

"I think there are a lot of people, men and women alike, who feel that way out there," she said. "The reality is that you don't have to love everything about this president, but you sure can love the direction that he's taking this country." She rattled off his policies, from tax cuts to national security. She landed on the age-old question "Are you better off than you were four years ago?"

"You might not love everything he tweets, but you never have to wonder what this president is thinking. He's very transparent," she said, days after critics and supporters alike cringed at a tweet he lobbed at the "squad" of new Democratic congresswomen.

"I think because he is unconventional, he's been incredibly effective," she said. "You don't have to follow all of the old rules in Washington, D.C. He's beholden only to the American people, not to lobbyists, not to special interest groups."

The campaign's decision to kick off Women for Trump in Montgomery County, a suburban Philly county that supported Clinton in 2016, was no accident. It plans to make inroads with married suburban women, because it has to to win reelection in 2020.

For two decades, married women have gravitated toward Republican presidential candidates.

In fact, Republican candidates have won the married women vote since 1996, said Brauer: "In 2012, Romney beat Obama with this demographic 53% to 46%. However, this trend changed in 2016. Clinton was able to edge out Trump with married women 49% to 47%–still a decent showing for Trump running against the first woman major candidate."

Brauer said evidence of Trump's suburban-women voter problem emerged in the results of last year's midterm elections and in part comes from his uncensored use of Twitter. "Some of this erosion is due to his brash comments about and to prominent women and racial minorities, and some is due to his policy stances, such as his efforts to repeal health care reforms and the treatment of migrant families on the border," he said.

Given all that, it is a smart and critical initiative for the Trump team to begin specifically courting women's votes, especially in places like suburban Philadelphia. And Lara Trump's visit was the beginning of the initiative, said Brauer.

"These suburbs have a strong demographic of married women who tend to vote Republican but are willing to vote Democratic for the right candidates. So their votes must be earned," said Brauer.

The strongest message for married women is probably an economic one: This demographic knows firsthand the struggles of maintaining a career and raising a family, especially to give their children more opportunities than they had.

"The message should be all about the booming economy, especially low unemployment/high job opportunities, increasing wages/salaries, tax cuts and the ability to retire with the growth of 401(k)s," said Brauer. "They need to be convinced their families and children will have a better economic life with a second Trump term."

If the Trump team can successfully make that argument, then perhaps these women will overlook the president's foibles and their disparities with him, said Brauer. "It is an effort worth undertaking."

# Rural America, 'Romanticism' and Open Minds

*July 30, 2019*

ACCIDENT, Maryland–Hours before the festivities began, generations of families were lining up along U.S. Route 219, which is Main Street in this Garrett County town. Armed with coolers of ice, folding chairs and old blankets, and dressed in colorful patriotic clothing, they came to watch the 100-year-old homecoming parade that celebrates their community and the bold beginning of our independence.

Anticipation, that sweet pang of excitement and eagerness that's becoming less common in an age of instant gratification, was tangible as nostalgia swept the old and novelty thrilled the young.

A meaningful silence filled the crowd as the American Legion color guard of veterans spanning World War II to today's conflicts crested Route 219 and made their way along Main Street. A wave of applause and salutes greeted the men who made the sacrifice to serve first their country in their youth and then their community in their maturity.

Following them were scores of floats, fire equipment, local bands, scout troops, church groups, the Rotary Club, beauty pageant winners, plenty of livestock and the all-important volunteers, who tossed out penny candy to the gleeful young children.

Accident, Maryland, is not much different from many small towns that dot our countryside. It's got an odd name (yes, based on an accident), great trout fishing along the creek named after a bear, and just enough small businesses to provide a family's essentials (plus any sweet tooth, pizza craving or appetite for fresh, locally made cheese).

This isn't the story of rural life you'll read in much of the media. "I spent a lot of my vacation driving around rural areas, through NC, KY, and TN," wrote Vox.com blogger Dave Roberts. "My impression: horrible land use, bland, ticky-tacky strip-mall architecture, & economic decay. I feel compassion for those people but I have zero time for romanticism about US rural life."

But Mike Koch and Pablo Solanet don't romanticize about their lives in Accident. The married couple are Washington, D.C., expats. Koch worked in housing finance for 22 years, and Solanet was a sought-after Argentine-trained chef. They gradually eased out of Beltway life beginning in 2002, permanently departing a few years ago.

FireFly Farms, their bustling cheese business, is lined with paradegoers on the day of the homecoming. Despite their exquisite, locally made goat cheeses appearing on the coveted shelves of Whole Foods, Wegmans and Zabar's and served in dishes in some of the finest restaurants in New York and Washington, the men remain grounded and committed to their rural enterprise.

Koch said: "When we first started the business, Pablo was the original cheesemaker, the original herd manager. He really put his heart and soul, while I continued to work because, as you probably know, starting a farm-based business, the money just doesn't roll in. So, it was necessary to make sure we could sustain ourselves."

They are also deeply committed to their rural community. Koch said: "On election night 2016, we stopped watching the national news, and Pablo and I made the decision to focus on our community: Do we know the county commissioners? Do we go to the chamber of commerce annual membership dinner? Do we know about what's hot in Garrett County politics and what people would like to see in terms of improvements in recycling? Do we know Mayor Carlson of Accident, Maryland? Do we know Ruth Ann who runs town hall?"

That additional investment in community (outside of working with six local farms for their fresh goat milk and employing over 20 locals) has been, in a word, remarkable.

Koch dismisses the typical stereotypes hurled at rural people, saying: "It's no secret that Pablo and I are married and we're gay. It's never brought up. What they care about is: Are you contributing to the community? Are you creating jobs? Are you behaving like a responsible citizen? And the red/blue stuff? Well, people don't obsess about that in the way society assumes they do."

With the exception of a few years in Florida, Glen Maust has called Accident home. The hardworking entrepreneur who has both a construction company and a 25-unit apartment building fulfilled a dream last year when he opened the Rolling Pin Bakery with his wife.

On doughnut day, which is three days a week, the aroma tempts the pedestrians to dive into the bakers' family legacy; she is Mennonite and is using the same recipe her grandmother taught her as a child. There are also sandwiches, gobs, cookies, muffins and anything else you need to satisfy a sugary craving.

The father of six, Maust employs 15 locals including his son. He knows the challenges of rural life and embraces them: "Our town has had its up and downs, but we are definitely a prosperous, growing little town, but not so much that we're not in danger of getting a Walmart anytime soon."

It is a pretty open-minded town, said Maust: "I would say that we still would be a fairly conservative town, and most conservatives are open-minded. Certainly some aren't, but then there's some liberals that are so open-minded that their brains fall out."

"I think maybe the town of Accident is kind of a happy medium," he said.

# Rats Infest Our Cities, but There Are Bigger Barriers to a Better Life

*August 6, 2019*

GARY, Indiana–If you want to know the true state of a city, drive through all of it, not just the pretty parts where politicians line the streets with bike lanes and lavish developers who have deals to build by stadiums and riverfronts.

Here in this Indiana manufacturing town, there are hollowed-out neighborhoods, abandoned homes and boarded-up businesses lining U.S. Route 20 right beside well-kept homes whose owners are trying to restore dignity and stability to their home and community.

When President Trump took a swipe at Rep. Elijah Cummings of Maryland's 7th Congressional District and called the district filthy and rat-infested, the reaction ranged from cries of racism to a defense of rodents by the Baltimore Sun: "Better to have a few rats than to be one."

Lost in the outrage is the fact that there are rats in our largest cities, but there are also deep and profound issues plaguing the African Americans who live in cities like Baltimore and Gary: generational poverty, gun violence, gang wars and the collapse of the family. These cities suffer from a sense of despair and feeling stuck, not that different from rural or post-industrial regions in this country where generational poverty, lack of resources or lack of opportunity have led to high rates of opioid addiction, suicide and family collapse.

Most of America's challenges are not easily or fairly categorized by base-level demographics, such as race and geography, said Bruce Haynes, vice chairman of public affairs for the public relations firm Sard Verbinnen & Co. "They are primarily challenges created by the loss of adherence to values and the lack of access to opportunities," he said.

Instead of skin color and geography, the most powerful boundaries of isolation and forms of segregation today are drawn along the lines of marriage and faith: barriers to economic opportunity, community resources and quality education.

"Where we find a lack of commitment to, and resultant abandonment of, the traditional institutions of our society such as our schools, businesses, communities, churches and families is where we find generational poverty, violence, addiction and lack of opportunity," he said.

Politicians instead look at places like inner-city Baltimore and rural West Virginia and use divisive attacks that both trivialize and tribalize us. "These politics fail us all and exact a high cost," said Haynes. "We are all made in the image of God and we are all in need of Grace, not just from God but from each other. We all deserve an opportunity to have work, dignity and be a part of a family and a community. When people become isolated–by choice or by loss–from these most traditional and basic institutions of our society, they fall into a desperate cycle of despair from which it can be incredibly difficult to recover."

The best hope we might have is for politicians to return to one of our founding virtues: honesty.

Instead of using these problems as political sledgehammers to crush their opponents, they should use them to draw us together, rally us as a people around the need to reinstate the values that made our society great, and support institutions with the public and private resources necessary to flourish in challenged communities.

"That is the ultimate promise of populism, but it has historically always been an empty promise because it has been used to divide," said Haynes.

Perhaps a leader will come along one day who will worry less about finding ways to get the have-nots to hate the haves; not condemn us for our privilege or despair, or divide us by demographics; and instead focus on how to create more opportunity, prosperity and community for all, regardless of circumstance.

# The Death of a Local Newspaper Rocks America to Its Core

*August 13, 2019*

YOUNGSTOWN, Ohio–When the press stops rolling at The Vindicator this month, a lingering question will once again taunt the residents of the Mahoning Valley: How much collapse can one region take?

The family-owned newspaper announced in June–just days after celebrating its 150th anniversary–that it is permanently ceasing production on Aug. 31. Started in 1869 just months after Ulysses S. Grant was sworn into office, it has been run by the descendants of William F. Maag ever since he purchased it midway through Grover Cleveland's first term.

The closure will cost 144 employees and 250 carriers their jobs and comes just weeks after the General Motors Lordstown plant down the road turned out the lights, leading to thousands of job losses.

It is one of a series of gut punches that has dented this area's spirit since the collapse of the steel industry in September 1977. But losing a local newspaper feels like a bigger blow than most.

"Newspapers are the watchdogs who hold our civic institutions accountable and act as a cheerleader for the unique fabrics in our society," Democratic presidential candidate Rep. Tim Ryan, the congressman who represents this region, told The New York Post.

As a young high school football star, Ryan enjoyed glowing coverage in The Vindicator. And as an elected official, he has felt the sting of its criticism.

"We've had our share of tensions, and they certainly have held me accountable, but that is their job–to be that check on government–and I cannot imagine our community without them," he said.

Closures like The Vindicator's are sadly more common than ever across the country, as old-school newsrooms struggle to compete with digital operations that aggregate web content but lack editorial oversight or seasoned reporters who have a deep understanding of their local area.

In the past 15 years, the country has lost 1,800 local news organizations, according to a report by the University of North Carolina Center for Innovation and Sustainability in Local Media. Half of the country's 3,143 counties have just one newspaper to cover sprawling, often isolated territories, while nearly 200 counties have no newspaper at all, the report said.

"A local newspaper is to a community what a central nervous system is to a body," said Paul Sracic, a political science professor at Youngstown State University. "Like the nerves in our body, the newspaper transmits vital and non-vital information throughout the community."

And without that, it's very difficult for a community to maintain its sense of self.

At the local school, Becky Ford has used The Vindicator (formerly known as The Youngstown Vindicator) as a resource for the American history and social studies classes she teaches. She also relies on it to stay connected with her community. "For us, it was like our New York Times," Ford said. "Sports, features, local social clubs, volunteer activities, class reunions ... you name it, they did it. If you called The Vindicator and asked (them) to be at your event, they were at your event taking pictures."

High school athletes, in particular, will suffer from a lack of coverage, said Rick Shepas, athletic director of Youngstown city schools.

It will be "devastating for the kids and their families not to have The Vindicator write those daily articles about the student-athlete's accomplishments both on and off the field," he said.

After 150 years of chronicling the Ohio Valley, beginning with the Reconstruction and followed by the Industrial Revolution, two World Wars, a Great Depression, civil rights, a moon landing, the Vietnam War, Watergate, 9/11 and the rise of populism, it is hard to believe that The Vindicator is no more.

Although the internet is a great source of information, the virtual communities that exist on sites like Reddit aren't local or even identifiable.

Youngstown Mayor Jamael Tito Brown worries that the disruption caused by the paper's closure won't stop at the city line.

"This is a problem for our whole country," Brown said. "Communities suffer when local journalism closes up shop, and we lose our vitality and connection to each other when that door closes for the last time."

He adds, "The bigger problem is: How are we going to stop those doors from closing here–or anywhere?"

# The Perils of Trading Social Interaction for Social Media

*August 20, 2019*

ESTES PARK, Colorado–I often say that what happens on Twitter isn't a reflection of American life in the real world.

The facts mostly back that up. Last month, a Pew survey showed only about 22% of U.S. adults say they use Twitter. Twitter users skew younger, identify more as Democrats, are more educated and have more money than the other 78% who don't use it.

Experiences back that up as well. Halfway through a 16-state back-road trip across the country, I've had many people–both conservative and liberal–tell me that if they use Twitter, they don't use the social media platform in the way we assume they do.

They mostly observe. And what they see often makes them not want to jump into the discussion.

They also worry about how Twitter is used as a blunt-force weapon to punish those with unpopular views, diminishing a healthy discourse to debate differences. They are not wrong.

The Twitter experience gives people pause about expressing their views on anything, because anything these days, even a cat video, is just one keystroke from becoming a political hot potato.

This is not a small problem. We should be able to have a normal political debate. America was founded partly in a fight to express political disagreement. Many of us have not-too-distant ancestors who escaped oppressive societies, kingdoms, dictators and/or countries so they and their children could express dissent. And yet, social media has become a place where it can be downright dangerous to do so.

What have we created? We have been given a technological gift, and we've abused it in the worst possible way. Social media might have allowed us to engage in the kind of open discourse that is the lifeblood of democracy.

Instead, said Youngstown State University political science professor Paul Sracic, we are using it to censor ideas we don't like or that we think are wrong: "The problem is that we don't understand democracy. Democracy is not about truth. Democracy, or voting, is what we do when we don't know the truth."

The Catholic Church is not a democracy, and that's because it claims to possess religious truth. When it comes to questions of doctrine, voting would be a form of heresy. But whenever we don't know the truth, we want to engage as many voices as possible.

"Nowadays, however, both extremes on the political spectrum feel that they have absolute truth. So, our political wars have become like the old religious wars, and 'error has no rights,'" said Sracic.

"So instead of informing us, social media makes us more ignorant by denying us the right to be wrong," he lamented.

If we are not exposed to contradictory ideas from which we might learn because we are afraid of either being ruined by a social media attack or so turned off by the vitriol and intolerance against opposing views, we will eventually hibernate within a tribe that looks and feels closest to us.

And we become our lesser selves because of it.

The truth is it is only by confronting and answering arguments against our own positions that we can thoroughly understand our own beliefs.

Sracic points to a line by G.K. Chesterton: "It is not bigotry to be certain we are right; but it is bigotry to be unable to imagine how we might possibly have gone wrong."

Nothing is new under the sun; silencing our political enemies is a very old political problem. What is new is how many people are trying to silence you.

Or at least place just enough fear in you that you choose not to engage.

Writing back in 1787, in the first of what we now know as the Federalist Papers, Alexander Hamilton warned his readers: "So numerous indeed and so powerful are the causes, which serve to give a false bias to the judgment, that we upon many occasions, see wise and good men on the wrong as well as on the right side, of questions of the first magnitude to society. This circumstance, if duly attended to, would furnish a lesson of moderation of those, who are ever so much persuaded of their being in the right, in any controversy."

Sracic said Hamilton also cautioned, "in politics as in religion, it is equally absurd to aim at making proselytes by fire and sword. Heresies in either can rarely be cured by persecution."

The larger question becomes: What if Twitter does become real life? What if we were to confront strangers in person daily the way many people do on the platform?

Imagine walking down the street wearing a T-shirt with your favorite band on it and having someone get in your face because he had a bad experience at one of the band's concerts. Or drinking coffee that someone says once offended him politically and experiencing him publicly accuse you of being a bigot. Or being mobbed by dozens of people for smiling at a joke a comedian makes because they find the jokes offensive.

Twitter is a community you join. Throughout our young history, joining and forming associations and communities was an American pastime observed with awe by French historian Alexis de Tocqueville, who noted not just that we are forever forming them but that our society and the forming of our country greatly benefited from them.

So, does our society benefit from Twitter? Or do we need to amend Tocqueville's conclusions about the virtue of American-made communities?

There are no easy answers here. As someone who sees a diverse variety of human interaction both online and in person, my best observation is this: When we replace the human-level communities we thrive in–such as religion, civic responsibility, education and volunteerism–with communities online that give us a false sense of power, we are heading down the path of failure.

## Small-Business Men Get a Front-Row Seat for Everyday Life

*August 27, 2019*

WAUPACA, Wisconsin–In another lifetime, the Park Motel and Supper Club sat along U.S. Route 10 and enjoyed both local patrons and famished travelers looking for a good homemade meal and a place to rest on this highway connecting Bay City, Michigan, to Fargo, North Dakota (including a 62-mile ferry ride across Lake Michigan).

Over the years, the motel housed the sequestered jurists for the trial of Jennifer Patri, the woman who claimed that horrendous abuse at the hands of her husband led her to shoot him with a rifle, bury his body in the basement of the farmhouse and then set it all on fire.

The motel also housed Weyauwega farmers after a train derailment and allowed vendors to sell custom-made stained glass windows. But mostly, it offered all sorts of families visiting the Midwest an affordable place to spend a night.

And the spacious supper club attached to the motor lodge became a place for locals to take their families or take a date for a special dinner and a night out on the town.

Today, the Park Motel is closed. A fire several years ago caused the Murphys, the current owners, to shutter the lodging part of the business. They kept the supper club, though, and it's now called the Courtside Sports Bar.

And if you are smart, you will be there for dinner every Friday for fish fry. You just have to try really hard to find the bar, now that the bustling highway it once sat along cut their access off when it was widened years ago.

"I know it is difficult. I'm always happy when people can find it," said Karen Murphy. During the day, she is an accountant; at night, she can be found in the kitchen preparing for the fish fry.

"We make our own breading, and we don't pre-bread. We bread to order. We also make our own tartar sauce," she said.

The place is packed, and the crowd is motley. Three bikers and a family with three young children sit at the bar eating dinner. In the back where the salad bar is, a long table is filled with Korean War veterans and their wives, as well as several couples young and old enjoying walleye or trout or bass with sides of coleslaw and mounds of french fries.

Murphy says the highway situation "somewhat" hurts them, but it is the quality of food, the cheery service and the lack of wait time that brings people back. "There's a few places that, you know, you have to wait an hour or two hours to get fish," she says. "You never have to wait at our place. ... We're never really swamped. We get the food out pretty fast."

Murphy, like small-business owners in every corner of the country, said that despite always being tired, she loves the work. She loves the people she meets, the food she makes and the sense of being a draw to her community: "I enjoy going out into the dining room or out to the bar and talking to people 'cause that's, I feel, what brings people back."

This is a common story to hear from small-business men.

"If we don't have it, you don't need it," said Steve Boris of Cataract Mart, about two hours west of Waupaca. He's not wrong. He's got fresh local produce, hardware, groceries, grilling supplies, very popular homemade sandwiches and just about everything you need in a pinch, all neatly stacked inside the compact roadside building.

He's been a small-business owner for 41 years. Before launching this general store 21 years ago, he owned a Kentucky Fried Chicken franchise, a candymaking business and a catering business. It's the general store, though, he says he loves the most: "I love people, love working with people, love talking to people. And general stores are really central to rural areas."

"We're 12 miles from one town and 16 miles from another town, and we're all in the country," he added. "We have a lot of people that need a lot of stuff. We've got everything, groceries, beer. We're the post office. We have hardware."

This glimpse is extraordinary, just because we get a glimpse into these two Wisconsinites' ordinary, daily lives. There was no talk of politics or cultural wokeness either with them or between them and their customers. No one was boycotting them for having found out they had donated to some candidate or demanding they take a stand on some social justice issue.

They just were. And their customers just were. And everything was OK.

Sometimes a day in a life of someone else in someplace else reminds us that the forces you thought were ripping us apart haven't. And that at our very core, despite whatever challenges we face in our daily lives, and despite the national daily drumbeat that portrays us as divided over everything, we as a country are doing pretty OK.

# Cancel Culture Isn't Real Life—Yet

*September 3, 2019*

CLEAR SPRING, Maryland–It's 7 a.m. at the McDonald's drive-thru just off U.S. 40, and a cheery freckle-faced server emerges from the side door to deliver an order to a car parked in a waiting area.

"Heeeere's your Egg McMuffin, young lady," she announces with a broad smile.

For the next half-hour, a flurry of travelers and regulars grab a quick bite on the run or settle in with friends to trade their thoughts on the Blazers, the local high school football team, and the team's new coach. Small talk about the weather, various aches and ailments, and their community also fills the fast food restaurant.

Often, when people think about McDonald's ownership, they picture a big corporation located miles from its restaurants, with the CEO disconnected from the communities he serves and the people who work for the corporation. But the truth is most of the restaurants that sit under the golden arches are franchises owned by people like Stan Neal, who owns this McDonald's along with 20 others in Maryland and West Virginia.

Neal got his start as a 15-year-old flipping burgers at a nearby Hagerstown franchise. He not only stayed rooted to his community but also gives back to it through donations to the local school, scholarship monies and free meals for the needy. A few years ago, when he owned a motel, he gave out free rooms after a historic flood hit the area.

Neal and the thousands of McDonald's franchise owners across the country are not the kind of big corporate bosses pictured by activists and critics. This complicates the increasingly hysterical and frequent boycotts of corporations perceived to have violated some woke dogma.

"People want to make a statement by boycotting corporations because of the political views of the ownership," said Tom Maraffa, professor emeritus at Youngstown State University. "In the case of fast food companies, often the local restaurant which would be the subject of the boycott is a franchisee who may have held the franchise years before the current political climate and may even have political views that differ from those corporate leadership."

Never mind the actual employees.

Last week, Olive Garden was targeted–falsely–as being a corporate supporter of President Trump. Last month, a boycott was called against Equinox and SoulCycle because owner Stephen Ross was hosting a fundraiser for Trump. Several weeks ago, Nike pulled patriotically inspired shoes with the Betsy Ross flag because brand ambassador Colin Kaepernick objected to the design, causing people on both sides to proclaim their intent to boycott the brand.

It's all so exhausting.

The outrage mob has become such a parody that stand-up comedian Dave Chappelle took a poke at the culture in his new Netflix special. He did an impersonation and asked the audience to name the target.

He said: "Duh! Hey! Dur! If you do anything wrong in your life, duh, and I find out about it, I'm gonna try to take everything away from you, and I don't care what I find out. It could be today, tomorrow, 15, 20 years from now. If I find out, you're f---ing, duh, finished!"

While the audience began yelling that he was impersonating Trump, Chappelle instead pointed directly back at them and said: "That's you! That's what the audience sounds like to me. That's why I don't be coming out and doing comedy all the time, because y'all ... is the worst motherf---ers I've ever tried to entertain in my f---ing life."

In other words, it is not just corporations that are being boycotted or canceled. It's individuals who are being canceled by culture and the journalist class. This past week, The Washington Post ran a piece in which it flagrantly smeared author J.D. Vance, absurdly labeling his laments about the falling birthrate in America as white supremacy.

Maraffa argues that however visible this cancel culture and boycott fever are, they have not found their way into American life in a broad and meaningful way. When they do, it often backfires.

Consider the case of Chick-fil-A, when the social justice crowd went into full protest against the Georgia-based company for the faith of its leadership. Despite hundreds of protests, and government bodies in San Antonio, Texas, and Buffalo, New York, banning Chick-fil-A restaurants in their airports, nothing has gotten in the way of the company's unmatched growth.

Maraffa worries about what things would look like, though, if real life were to become like Twitter. What if boycott lists were something people carried on their person or in their smartphone?

"It's not beyond the realm of possibility," he warns. "Performance wokeness is a plague, and we should do everything we can to avoid it from seeping into our daily lives."

## It Will Take Hometown Heroes to Fix Broken Towns

*September 10, 2019*

EAST LIVERPOOL, Ohio–Greg Bricker is tired of his community looking through the rearview mirror to an idyllic past, rather than looking forward and trying to plot a better course.

He feels this rearview mindset dominates his town, especially the local government.

So after missing the statewide deadline for getting on the Nov. 5 ballot, Bricker went down to the Columbiana County Board of Elections to register as a write-in candidate for mayor of East Liverpool.

Outside of his wife, Katie, he didn't even tell his family. The rest of his family "found out when they read in the local paper," he says with a smile.

Street after street in the neat grid of East Liverpool is filled with stunning turn-of-the-century buildings that are all boarded up.

East Liverpool was once the pottery capital of the world. More than 300 pottery companies competed here to win business all around the country. But since the 1960s, East Liverpool has been plagued with massive population loss and a fentanyl crisis that made national headlines. This is the town where, in 2016, a grandmother and her companion were found overdosing in their car, while her 4-year-old grandson looked on helplessly from a car seat.

Since then, the opioid crisis has ebbed, something Dr. Bob Walker, who stops to chat with Bricker, attributes to heightened social services. But the town continues to bleed.

"I went to a city council meeting this past week," Bricker says, "and they were touting two things that made me realize even more how much we need to change our goals for this city: how we gained 22 people since the last census, and tearing down some businesses and houses that were abandoned."

Bricker is at the deli counter of Bricker's Cafeteria on 6th Street. His uncle Don is behind the counter, putting out fresh-baked lemon and coconut pies with mile-high towers of meringue.

The place is part deli, part grocery store and part old-time cafeteria. Bricker, now 33, worked here throughout his childhood and during summer in his college years.

He married Katie McIlvain, a girl from high school whose family owns the nearby Homer Laughlin China Company. She serves as the marketing manager of this iconic American pottery company that makes the colorful Fiestaware dinnerware. It also makes china used in both the finest restaurants and the coziest diners in the country.

When the Brickers first married, Greg Bricker hung up his shingle (he is a CPA) in downtown East Liverpool, and they both commuted from their home in the Squirrel Hill neighborhood of Pittsburgh.

"But we both wanted not to just come home; we wanted to make a difference in our hometown," he says. Since they've moved back, Bricker has become more and more determined to "do something."

He recently bought one of those old buildings to place his business.

He meets monthly with a handful of other civic-minded people who stayed in town and talks about a strategy to help East Liverpool. "Finally, I decided the only way I can bring change is to take the risk and run for mayor," he says.

Bricker is the kind of millennial whom rural places or post-industrial towns dream of bringing back. He's offering ideas and a little personal risk in an effort to lift the town up. He is young, fearless, tactical and dedicated. He serves on five boards in the city including at the Y, the local hospital and the Rotary Club. Towns like East Liverpool need an abundance of Bickers.

He says: "We cannot continue to hold on to that dream of some big employer coming to town and saving us. We've done that for a generation, and that dream has never come true. Instead we need to work on attracting small businesses to our city and working with them as partners for all of our success."

That kind of vibrancy will then make them more attractive to a larger company, he says.

Bricker faces incumbent Mayor Ryan Stovall and at-large councilman Brian Kerr. His challenge may not be as quixotic as you may think; of the 10,000 people who live in the city limits, just over 2,000 voted for Stovall four years ago. In a three-way race, Bricker's quest is far from impossible.

"I knocked on 300 doors last week from a voter list," he says. "Then I just decided to throw the list away. I am going to knock on every door and tell the people some of my plans for the city and ask them how I can best earn their vote."

The first thing he'd like to do is reduce the 20% storefront vacancy rate downtown: "I have to be able to sell this as a place to live and do business. That's our first challenge. It's one I know I can do."

# The Crackers and Frackers Could Hold the Keys to 2020

*September 17, 2019*

MONACA, Pennsylvania–All Darrin Kelly wanted for the energy workers in Western Pennsylvania was that the Democratic presidential hopefuls would talk to them before going to war against shale.

That opportunity slipped away last Friday when Elizabeth Warren joined Bernie Sanders in calling for a total fracking ban.

"On my first day as president, I will sign an executive order that puts a total moratorium on all new fossil fuel leases for drilling offshore and on public lands. And I will ban fracking–everywhere," Warren tweeted.

"It is disappointing that any national candidate would not come in here and want to talk to the men and women of this area first before unilaterally making that decision," said Kelly, a charismatic Pittsburgh firefighter who is also the head of the powerful and influential Allegheny Fayette Labor Council, which represents workers stretching from Pittsburgh to the borders of Maryland and West Virginia.

The rest of the Democratic hopefuls will follow suit, with the possible exceptions of Joe Biden and Ohio Rep. Tim Ryan. At least, that's the prediction of Keystone College political science professor Jeff Brauer.

"The natural gas industry employs well over 40,000 people just in this region alone," Kelly said. "Countless more indirectly, providing economic opportunity for generations of families and communities that had been hollowed out by the demise of manufacturing and coal in this area."

Donald Trump won Pennsylvania with just over 40,000 votes in 2016.

Kelly doesn't think he is entitled to the presidential candidates' time. He just knows what happens when the energy labor force in Western Pennsylvania isn't behind the Democratic nominee.

"You cannot win the presidency if you are a Democrat without Pennsylvania," Brauer reminds bluntly.

Democrats have won Pennsylvania in past presidential years because of outsized margins in Philadelphia, Pittsburgh and their suburbs. That support has been declining since Bill Clinton won 28 of the state's 67 counties in 1996.

Barack Obama won 13 of the 67 counties in 2012.

Trump's magic came in rural and post-industrial counties such as Luzerne and Erie, but most importantly in the populous counties around Pittsburgh, where shale is king and fracking is seen as the second coming of the steel industry.

They may look like ordinary construction cranes to someone unfamiliar with the history of this region. But if you're from here, they look like something different. Building the ethane cracker plant, each of these cranes looks like a new colossus rising from the ashes of yesterday's despair.

Building the plant has brought in 6,000 good-paying jobs, with more to come. Ultimately, there will be 600 permanent jobs at the plant, with industry analysts predicting triple that amount in supporting industries.

Jobs postings are everywhere touting opportunities, no matter the skill level–high school education, trade school certificate, chemists, engineers, information technology, labor. If you reliably turn up for work, there is likely a career for you in the oil and gas industry.

"And if you think our workers don't care for the environment or climate change you are wrong," said Kelly. "They are the ones not only working in the industry, but they live here, play here, raise their kids here, hunt, fish, boat, ski, swim, and hike. They want to be in a responsible industry," he said.

The high tides of the frackers and crackers will be offset by the sinking tide of the broader U.S. economy, experts predict. "We're going to probably enter at least a little bit of an economic downturn," Brauer warns, "which is the natural part of the cycle. And it's probably not going to be the greatest timing for President Trump since that's his strength."

"But if the Democrats continue to make these arguments and push these issues which are going to hurt the economy and these key states, then it plays right into Trump's narrative," he adds with a twist.

Brauer suggested Trump could easily argue: "This is part of the cycle and what's going to happen, but would you rather have me, who's going to have less regulations and not wipe out entire industries and try to build back the manufacturing base and try to get jobs to come back in the United States, or you have a Democrat who is so far to the Left, who's willing to get rid of entire industries because of some environmental concerns that can be addressed, without destroying the whole industry?"

That's not a tough question for most Western Pennsylvanians. But it poses a tough question for Biden and the other 2020 Democrats.

# Repurposing 'America's Hometown'

*September 24, 2019*

OAKDALE, Pennsylvania–Some towns die hard. This one nearly did.

The Aetna Chemical Corp. plant exploded 101 years ago, leveling most of the town, killing nearly 200 people, maiming hundreds more. Some body parts landed nearly a mile away.

The horrifying news ran across the front page of every newspaper in the country, with reports of carnage and photos of a demolished landscape in which buildings and trees were leveled.

That's the most notable thing to ever happen in Oakdale, which since its inception has been fondly called "America's hometown." Way back when, it was a quaint agriculture community, the farmers of which were skeptical when the powerful Pennsylvania Railroad's main line to St. Louis and Chicago cut through their pastures in the years before the Civil War.

Thus, Oakdale became part of the connection of the East to the Midwest, which is why Aetna located its plant there. The railroad is also why Kinsey Electric located there 15 years after the blast. But after the railroad left in the late '70s, bringing with it the commerce, connection, shoppers and laborers, America's hometown again faced an uncertain future.

Some ruins of the Aetna plant are still visible if you work your way through the weeds. The old Kinsey Electric warehouse stands on the same road. That building somehow cast a spell on a local woman named Whitney Jurgovan.

"I live three minutes from the building, and I drove by it all of the time," she said. "I love old industrial buildings," she gushed, praising "their windows and their rusty amazingness."

"One day, the doors were open. It was a rainy, freezing November day, and I said: 'I'm just gonna stop there. I don't know what's going on there, so I'm just gonna stop,'" the petite blonde said.

"There was a gentleman in there. His name was Claude. He rented a room inside the building for a custom pet food company. He was obviously taken back by why I was there and what I wanted. I said, 'I want to do this thing here.'" This "thing" she wanted to do was to house a market there a couple of times a year, filling it with artisans, antique dealers, food trucks and coffee stands, with a wine and cheese party on the first night and a local band.

Everyone–except for her pragmatic engineer husband, Tony– thought she was a wee bit crazy. "Nobody understood until we had the first market what I was actually trying to do," said the former stay-at-home mom, who sold antiques on the side, mostly as a hobby.

In honor of the former inhabitant of the old warehouse, she named her enterprise the Kinsey Market and set to work cleaning up the old insulators, gears and grease stains from all the engines, motors and transformers that were once made there.

She initially rented the building from a very skeptical absentee owner, got some vendors, hoped the leaky roof would hold up and held her first market last year.

Over 1,000 people showed up, mostly from word of mouth, a Facebook post and a lot of praying.

The next market, four months later, nearly doubled that. The parking lot was filled with license plates not just from Pennsylvania but also Ohio, West Virginia and Maryland.

She had local high school kids directing parking in the old gravel lot, and her sons Jacob and Carter manning a food drive at the entrance as customers brought in canned goods for the local food bank.

Two years after her "crazy" idea, Whitney and her husband bought the old building for the cost of the back taxes. Since then, they've fixed the leaky roof, installed lovely bathrooms and hosted scores of community events, including wreath-making, a vintage motorcycle swap and several weddings.

Beyond that, she helped the community pick itself up once again.

At the diner in town (it is literally named "The Diner"), the hostess says when a Kinsey Market weekend is happening, they staff up. The next market is in a few days, and the hostess says, "We know our business will double."

By all accounts, this town should have died either with the explosions or when the trains stopped coming. Yet, out of the ashes of "American's Hometown," a young family found a way to bring life back to a place in a way that no big corporation could have.

Compared to the large monopolies we allow to control our every move–from our privacy to how we fly, drive, book our hotels and shop for everything we need–businesses like the Kinsey Market open us up to the very essence of localism and place.

This is an example of repurposing someone's past aspiration into a new one rather than leveling it or leaving it behind–all because Whitney saw "amazingness" in a rusty old warehouse.

# Old-School House Democrats Face Primary Challenges From Progressives Across the Country

*October 1, 2019*

PITTSBURGH–Jerry Dickinson is the Democrats' perfect House candidate–and not just on paper. Yes, he's young, accomplished, academic and a charismatic liberal outsider who supports the ideals of the Green New Deal, the impeachment of the president and can self-raise an impressive amount of cash for his candidacy. He is all of those things and more.

His only handicap is that he's running against a Democratic incumbent. That, however, is far less of an obstacle in this new era, when incumbency may not hold the weight among Democratic primary voters that it used to. Once Rep. Joe Crowley fell to Alexandria Ocasio-Cortez in 2018, primary season became incumbent-hunting season for eager liberals who had enough ambition and confidence and could run in safe Democratic districts.

Dickinson is that guy. Mike Doyle, the veteran congressman from Pittsburgh, is his target.

"Twenty-plus years is a long time in office," Dickinson says. "Look at the record. Is Doyle liberal enough to lead what is a safe, strongly Democratic district? The answer is no."

Dickinson describes what he thinks Pittsburgh deserves: "Think about the safe blue districts all across the United States, whose representatives take on the liberal mantle, who are loud. They are leaders. They stick their neck out on the issues that really, really do matter to liberals. That should be happening here. This is a post-industrial liberal enclave, which actually makes it in a unique position to actually be the leader on all major issues."

Doyle was first elected to office as a rare Democratic freshman in the Republican wave election year of 1994. He's lived through two redistrictings, but his seat is still based in Pittsburgh.

Doyle has never really faced much of a challenge either in a primary or a general election. The most iconic moment of his congressional career came during his time as head coach of the Democrats' congressional baseball team when he drew the team in from the practice field in prayer when news hit that the congressional Republicans' baseball team members were under attack on another practice field. His only controversy came in 2003 when his residence, at a home filled with Republican and Democratic members, came under scrutiny when it was revealed the landlord was a religious organization.

Doyle, a practicing Roman Catholic, said at the time of the living arrangement: "It's very ecumenical. We all pay for the food. We have common life experiences. We're also people of faith."

Dickinson, who is black, has a compelling life story. Separated as an infant from his biological parents by the Orphans' Court, Jerry was eventually fostered and then adopted into a "boisterous and loving home" parented by a white couple, Robert and Judy Dickinson. They ended up adopting eight children in total.

"Everyone's early childhood experiences shape your life in some way," Dickinson says. "It just so happens in mine was in this multiracial environment–and sometimes chaotic environment."

Dickinson smiles as he fondly talks about his family background and calls his father, Robert, one of his best friends. "He's a late-70s white man, you know? And even though I am a black man in America, we've just built this very neat relationship and deep bond."

History is certainly on Doyle's side, though, explains Kyle Kondik, managing editor of Sabato's Crystal Ball at the University of Virginia Center for Politics. "More than 98% of all House members who have sought renomination by their parties since the end of World War II have, in fact, been renominated."

Still, Doyle should not dismiss Dickinson. "One also would expect a handful to succeed in any given year," Kondik said, pointing to both Crowley and Republican Eric Cantor in 2014.

The Intercept reported last week that the chair of the Democratic Congressional Campaign Committee, Rep. Cheri Bustos, counted as many 111 primaries for her incumbent members, a higher-than-normal number as the Democratic Party struggled with the leftward trajectory of their new coalition, which is less white, more educated and youthful.

Dickinson left suburban Pittsburgh to attend the College of the Holy Cross, where he excelled both in the classroom and on the soccer field. He returned to practice law and later to teach it at the University of Pittsburgh.

"I realized it was time to step up and be the one to actually take on this fight for this region and be the strong voice it needs."

In a different era, a 32-year-old liberal assistant law professor probably would have remained on the sidelines. But in today's climate, Dickinson has jumped into the fray.

# Our 90-Second Culture

*October 8, 2019*

A lot can happen in 90 seconds.

In 2013, it took the flight attendants on Asiana Airlines Flight 214 only 90 seconds to evacuate nearly 300 people off of a plane that had crashed at San Francisco International Airport–despite their personal injuries and the flames and smoke in the cabin.

In February 2016, a high school senior named Jessica Fitzgerald saved her co-worker's life at the pizzeria where they worked when he went into cardiac arrest right after a pizza delivery. She pulled out her cellphone, dialed 911 and started performing chest compressions. From the moment she picked up that phone and found no pulse to the moment she detected a faint pulse after she started CPR, she had saved his life.

In a minute and a half, lives can be saved. And in that time, the headlines show us again and again, lives can also be shattered.

We have become a culture of the moment. It's not that we live in the moment; it's that we consume moments. And when we take in moments stripped of context, our assumptions and prejudices fill in the blanks.

In late January, it only took 90 seconds of a video of a group of white teenage boys from Covington Catholic High School in Kentucky wearing "Make America Great Again" hats for the video to become the symbol of everything that is wrong in America. The video passed from activists to journalists to commentators to the headlines, and the moment became a story.

It took weeks for the full story with the full video to come out. That passage of time helped permanently lodge the original, misleading story in the public mind. Once again, the moment became the "truth" and the truth was subordinated.

Last week, a middle school girl in Northern Virginia confessed she was lying to her family and authorities. The girl, who is black, had claimed that three white classmates at her private Christian school cut off her dreadlocks and taunted her looks by calling her hair both "nappy" and "ugly."

The story spread instantly and hit national headlines because Vice President Mike Pence's wife, Karen Pence, is a part-time art teacher at the school. The effort to link Pence to the incident was not subtle. Read the headlines and you would almost believe her teaching there is the reason the alleged attack happened.

In our culture today, a social media post can be considered the gospel truth without any intellectual value.

Why? Well, there are many explanations. The first is old-fashioned laziness. The second is there are a lot of people out there who desperately want confirmation that the other side isn't merely different or wrong but just plain evil and deserving of punishment.

The third reason: the sadistic entertainment value of watching a stranger get viciously punished or destroyed. It's not much different than when people cheered on the clash of gladiators in the Roman Colosseum, only without blood.

Reality TV, full of on-camera embarrassment and public shaming, was a precursor to what we see today.

The moral challenge for each of us is this: What do we do in the moment when we see something on social media that reinforces everything we want to be true? Do we type up something snarky and spread the story? Or do we be our own lie detector and make sure the entire story has been fleshed out?

It is easy to spread first and ask questions later; social media is plainly designed for us to execute that impulse.

What we do in the moment matters. It makes a difference what we do, not only to us but also to our family, co-workers, community, city, state and country.

In a world where lives can be saved or destroyed in a moment, we must be the culture we want and need and embrace our better angels.

# How Small Cities and Towns Can Right Their Ship

*October 15, 2019*

ERIE, Pennsylvania–Several large pieces of cobalt-blue glass panels bearing "Don't Give Up the Ship" and a bold likeness of Commodore Oliver Hazard Perry lay broken at the top of the third-floor stairs of the old Park Place building in the city's main square.

If ever there were a motto that exemplified a place and her people, it would be those five words Perry had stitched on a flag–words that inspired him over 200 years ago when he bore the flag in his unlikely defeat of the British at the Battle of Lake Erie.

Given everything this town has gone through–from her heyday as the industrial powerhouse of the Great Lakes to a city bleeding people, jobs and opportunity–finding this inspiring reminder in a building that used to produce "Carter's Little Liver Pills" brought into focus the city's effort at rebuilding.

John Persinger and Matt Wachter could live in any other city in the country and prosper quite nicely. Instead, the CEO and vice president of finance and development are the founding leaders of the Erie Downtown Development Corporation. They, along with Tim NeCastro, CEO of Erie Insurance, the city's largest employer, have committed themselves to not give up the ship but to stabilize and rebuild it.

All three men are standing along a row of century-old buildings on North Park Row. The bones are good, but the buildings have all seen better days. The three men are discussing the projects they already have underway. These are projects meant to spark a cultural and culinary center, which they hope will in turn lead to a citywide metamorphosis.

"This is Perry Square. This is the heart of downtown. It's often been called the 'beating heart,' but we're not sure how much it beats these days because there's not a whole lot of activity," he said of the boarded-up buildings and scant pedestrian activity.

Here's the odd thing: The moribund heart is surrounded by an arc of life. "UPMC Hamot campus is a few blocks away," Persinger explains, "where they (are) putting in a new $111 million patient tower."

There's more: "Erie Insurance employs 3,000 people right there. They're building a new office building. You can kind of see it over the tree line."

Erie Insurance has been here for 94 years. NeCastro jokes he hasn't been here for quite that long, but he is a son of Erie. "I was one of six kids. My father died when I was seven, and my mother found herself working as a waitress at three different places to keep food on the table. ...

"I walked to grade school here. I walked to high school, and I even walked to college," he said of his education at Gannon University.

NeCastro says he left for other opportunities after college but wanted to find his way home. That happened when an internal auditing job opened up at Erie Insurance. Twenty years later, he worked hard "and sometimes too much" to reach what they call the C-suite.

Except he's one of those CEOs who shop in the same grocery store as their employees and customers–and whose proverbial "C-suite" is street-level.

"The recovery of this city is extremely important to us at Erie Insurance because we're the largest employer here. If the city goes to hell in a handbasket, who's going to want to come work for us here?" he said.

This is where Persinger comes in.

In 2018, a few months after Persinger ran for mayor and lost, NeCastro was casting about in frustration, seeking a CEO to lead the Development Corporation.

"So I called him," NeCastro says of Persinger, "and said: 'You wanted to be mayor because you wanted to make a difference in the city. Well, what if you could make a big difference, but you don't have to worry about the police department, the fire department, the streets, the picking up the garbage, all that stuff that goes with it?'"

Persinger's reaction? "Go on ..."

"Now a year and some change later, the EDDC has become one of the first cities in the country to attract investment to an Opportunity Zone, a 2017 federal jobs act designed to spur investments in low-income communities," he explains.

They've purchased eight properties surrounding Perry Square and have raised over $30 million in financing for their projects, which include retail as well as downtown housing.

NeCastro is the kind of guy who takes 10 days off from work every August to make 1,800 meatballs for his parish's Italian festival. Persinger is the kind of guy who grew up in New York City and went to Harvard but decided to make Erie his home because of his summers here with his grandparents.

They are both the kind of people who are called to serve the community, which happens to include the poorest ZIP code in the state. These are the guys dedicated to not giving up the ship.

# Why Mark Zuckerberg Wants to Recruit Outside the Ivy League Liberal Bubble

*October 22, 1029*

Mark Zuckerberg wants you to know that Facebook strives for diversity in its workforce–and not just on the basis of race or gender. The CEO says he works hard to recruit people who attended a state school, are rooted to their local communities and come from traditional backgrounds.

"We certainly do," Zuckerberg said of his 40,000 mostly U.S.-based employees in an interview with the New York Post.

"There's a woman who runs our commerce product and is deeply religious," he said. "The person who runs policies of the company is quite a prominent Republican. So we have people from quite different views, which I think might be a little bit different from most of the other tech companies. That's something that I really focused on."

Big tech companies, sports entities, Hollywood and the media have all faced criticism in recent years for the lack of cultural diversity in their leadership roles. It's even a problem in the public sector. A whopping 40% of the 250 top American public sector decision-makers are Ivy League graduates, according to a National Journal survey. Only a quarter hold a graduate degree from a public university.

And boardroom members typically come from the elite ZIP codes of New York City, Washington, D.C., Silicon Valley and their surrounding areas. Zuckerberg himself is an example of the problem:

He grew up in the wealthy Westchester town of Dobbs Ferry and went to Harvard before dropping out to focus on Facebook.

That lack of representation from people who grew up in rural areas or Rust Belt cities–whose experiences include sitting in a pew on Sunday, getting a little dirt under their nails and owning a gun–has widened the cultural divide and led to our current polarized political discourse.

Why? Because typically, the people who decide what ad you see or how your news is delivered or what behavior is acceptable on and off a sports field are unfamiliar with life in the part of America derisively nicknamed "flyover country."

Zuckerberg says he views Facebook as a series of small communities where the average Joe can speak out just as powerfully as a prominent politician.

"We need to make sure that we're giving more power to the equal," he said, "not just reinforcing existing institutions that exist in society.

"I think that's really important for where we are today, to not fall into a monoculture. Real progress has always been made by individuals having a voice and changing many individual steps forward to improve their lives and communities."

Zuckerberg was in Washington for a speech at Georgetown University that was livestreamed from his personal Facebook page. He will also testify next week before the House Financial Services Committee about his cryptocurrency project, Libra.

He said his speech–in which he defined his peer group of high-tech companies as the "fifth estate," taking their place alongside traditional news media–was one he had been thinking about for a very long time.

"I thought it was important to give a full articulation of my views on free expression. Giving people a voice is so important, and it has been throughout history," he said.

During our interview, the seemingly aloof Zuckerberg, 35, was candid in talking about how important his own Jewish faith is to him and relaxed and funny in reflecting on how things have changed since he launched "The Facebook" in his dorm room in 2004.

Zuckerberg has certainly taken his lumps. For years, he has been blasted from all sides for Facebook's business practices–from making money on false ads to breaching the privacy of its users. Oftentimes, the Facebook CEO and his team have seemed locked in an ivory tower as they arrogantly battled these crises from on high.

With his speech and this interview, Zuckerberg is clearly trying to show his more human side, especially as he fights accusations from both sides of the political aisle. While Republicans insist that users and news with a more conservative bent have been censored on his platform, Democrats claim Facebook spreads political misinformation.

Recently, presidential candidate Sen. Elizabeth Warren took this to the next level, paying for a deliberately deceptive Facebook ad that read, in part, "Breaking news: Mark Zuckerberg and Facebook just endorsed Donald Trump for reelection." Her ad was a response to Trump's 2020 reelection campaign ads, which blasted Joe Biden and his son for corruption, charges they both deny. Zuckerberg has so far not removed any of the ads and has defended this policy.

"People worry, and I worry deeply, too, about an erosion of truth," Zuckerberg told The Washington Post. "At the same time, I don't think people want to live in a world where you can only say things that tech companies decide are 100% true."

Even in the face of a cancel culture and tribal political war, Zuckerberg believes that free speech is absolute, and he does not think private companies should censor politicians.

"The hardest threat to free expression comes from our culture itself," he told the New York Post. "Because democracy depends on people holding each other's right to express ourselves above our own desire to get our way in every debate that we have.

"And increasingly, it seems like a larger number of people are willing to put whatever political outcome they want above respecting other people's ability to express themselves and have a voice," he said.

"I think that that's really dangerous."

## Will the Democrats Miss Middle America Again?

*October 29, 2019*

COLUMBUS, Ohio–In the weeks, then months and now years after losing the presidential election in 2016, Hillary Clinton has repeatedly demonstrated in speeches and television interviews that she has no idea why she lost. She has blamed everything from racism to Russia, from the media to sexism, from deplorables to stubborn, backward-looking nostalgia.

Now she's out saying Trump's presidency is illegitimate and that she would defeat him again.

She has not visibly reflected on the effects of her position on guns, her anti-fossil fuel talk and her open embrace of globalism. She seemingly hasn't considered the political cost of living within the bubbles of Washington, New York and Hollywood.

Talk to Democrats today who live outside her bubble, those who either volunteered endless hours to help elect her or voted for her, and they will tell you that Clinton has no idea why she lost. Worse, they see their party going down the same road that led to her defeat four years ago, blaming white resentment, as well as Russia, the media, sexism and deplorables.

You don't have to look any further than the sound bites from this past week's Democratic debate or the recent town halls. Confiscating guns, banning fracking, hiking taxes, providing free health care to illegal immigrants and stamping out religious liberty were the promises Democrats made to compete for primary votes.

Here is what most of Trump's critics don't understand about why this new conservative populist coalition voted for Trump over not just Clinton but also 17 very qualified, distinguished, mostly establishment Republican candidates in the party's primary battle.

It was never about Trump. It was always about their communities. Trump was the symptom, not the cause.

These voters aren't going to budge. It's not that everyone who voted for him considers his first term a massive success that has improved America's economy and made us safer. It's that Democrats and never-Trump Republicans have done nothing to reflect on why they lost to this guy. They'd rather make fun of the voters–it is easier and makes for great sport on Twitter–than admit their contribution to this flee from normalcy.

Successful people, when trying to recover from a setback, ask themselves, "Well, what did I do wrong to get my job/my life in this predicament?"

Democrats and Never-Trump Republicans won't accept any blame for losing the public. Instead, they blame the public. They never exclaim, "Dear God! They picked him over us? Jeez, we've got some self-reflection to do."

Which leads us back to what we've seen on the debate stage the past few months from the Democratic presidential candidates. They–with the exception of Amy Klobuchar and sometimes Pete Buttigieg–clearly haven't learned why Clinton lost.

Elizabeth Warren certainly hasn't. The national press see her as a safe front-runner, largely because they find her a familiar character. They know someone in their personal or professional lives who is just like her: She's their neighbor, their relative, or like someone they were taught by in college. Warren's viewpoints are also familiar in the newsroom, to put it gently.

It's not the same out here.

Democrats have lost the rural areas and are unchallenged in the urban areas, said Paul Sracic, political science professor at Youngstown State University. "Klobuchar and Buttigieg seem to understand that raising middle-class taxes to pay for health care will be a big issue for these voters," he said of the suburban middle-class voters who could be available to a Democratic presidential nominee.

There's a healthy amount of middle-class suburban voters who are looking for an alternative to their current options. It appears only two on that stage understood the lessons of 2016 and 2018: the senator from a Midwest state and the mayor of a Midwest city.

The rest seem to be repeating the mistakes of the former senator from New York.

# The Bellwether House Race for 2020 Is in Western Pennsylvania

*November 5, 2019*

MT. LEBANON, Pennsylvania–Army combat veteran Sean Parnell kicked off his race as a Republican running for the U.S. House here at Pamela's Diner. It's within a stone's throw of the district office of Rep. Conor Lamb, the Democrat he's challenging for the 17th Congressional District seat in 2020.

"My plan for today is just to tell the voters who I am, give them a sense of what I stand for and just listen to them and figure out what they feel is important," said Parnell before he headed off to two other diners in the district in Beaver and Butler counties in the western and northern suburbs of Pittsburgh.

The district is made up of neatly trimmed upper-middle-class, left-leaning Allegheny County suburbs such as Mt. Lebanon, working-class Beaver County communities packed with labor families and fiscal conservatives and enough rural and exurban Butler County voters to make the whole district a smidge Republican-leaning.

Parnell spent his time talking mostly with customers, but before he left, he took a beeline to the kitchen to talk to the cooks and servers. "I worked at Smartie Arties as a busboy, then as a cook from the time I was 15 until I was 21," he said. "I know how hard that job is, and I just want to thank them."

Parnell was born in Pittsburgh's Oakland neighborhood and went to Greensburg Central Catholic High School in Westmoreland

County. While attending Clarion University, he watched events unfold on 9/11 and felt a call to duty to join the Army. His service began in Afghanistan in 2006, commanding a platoon called "the Outlaws," who were stationed near the Pakistani border.

The experience and his bravery there earned him two Bronze Stars–one for valor–and the Purple Heart, as well as a New York Times bestseller, "Outlaw Platoon," which captures in vivid detail his platoon's grueling 16 months spent engaging in endless firefights in the mountains of Paktika province to upend the Haqqani network.

Lamb, the scion of a western Pennsylvania Democratic dynasty, is a former federal prosecutor and Marine Corps officer. He narrowly won his first race, beating Republican Rick Saccone for a seat in the 18th Congressional District in a special election in the spring of 2018.

Lamb then chose to run in the 17th Congressional District after the controversial move by the state's majority-Democrat Supreme Court, which redrew all of the congressional lines in the middle of last year after it determined the seats were politically drawn to favor Republicans–only to turn around and redraw them to favor Democrats.

The next race pitted two incumbents against each other: Lamb and Republican Keith Rothfus. Rothfus lost the seat to Lamb last November by a whopping 12 percentage points.

Before Parnell's surprise jump-in, Lamb was thought to have an easy glide to the finish line next year. No one expected House Republicans to be able to recruit a quality candidate to run in any of the swing districts the GOP lost last year that placed them in the wilderness, let alone one in western Pennsylvania.

Kyle Kondik, managing editor of Sabato's Crystal Ball at the University of Virginia's Center for Politics, said the Army Ranger's joining the race is a good development for the GOP: "I think this makes the district more competitive than it was prior to Parnell entering the race."

Kondik moved the race from "Safe Democrat" to "Likely Democrat" the night before Parnell's announcement.

In 2018, Lamb was the center of the Democratic universe. He raised $9 million in the Democratic Party's effort to shine national attention on GOP vulnerabilities and hand Trump a House loss. Since

January of this year, Lamb has raised $740,000 and has $563,000 cash on hand.

As a candidate, Lamb ran on a moderating message and avoided any support for impeachment. He benefited largely from union family support, something his Republican opponents were unable to capitalize on in the same way Trump did when he won the district by 2.5 percentage points.

On Thursday, Lamb cast a yes vote for an impeachment inquiry of the president.

Since the beginning of the 116th Congress, Lamb has voted over 90% of the time against legislation backed by Trump, which is probably why Trump publicly urged Parnell to challenge Lamb when he was speaking at the Shale Insight conference in Pittsburgh last week.

"It looks like PA 17 is going to have a true race in 2020," said Jeff Brauer, political science professor at Keystone College. "This race very well could become a bellwether race that will draw national interest and attention."

In short, if Parnell is ahead or closing in on Lamb for the western Pennsylvania seat, then Trump will likely win the Keystone State at the top of the ticket. Democratic presidential candidates cannot win Pennsylvania without western Pennsylvanian support, and they cannot win the presidency without Pennsylvania.

Brauer noted that in Lamb's first two victories, he positioned himself as a moderate in an area where Trump garnered and maintains significant support. "Lamb avoided running against Trump as much as possible, and he even claimed that he liked Trump," Brauer said. "However, since taking office, Lamb's actions and voting record have been to the contrary, as he has been a highly reliable Democratic vote for the House majority."

This past week, Lamb voted with the Democrats on a Republican effort to prevent future presidents from banning fracking, a game-changing economic driver in western Pennsylvania.

"This time, Lamb will be running against a peer," said Brauer. "In his first two elections, he ran against older, less charismatic opponents with whom he was able to easily draw a contrast. Parnell is also a young, charismatic millennial, as well as a veteran."

Brauer said Parnell can also run as a Washington outsider, as he hasn't run for office before. "Therefore, he can contrast himself to the Lamb family political dynasty. In many ways, Lamb will meet his match with Parnell," he said.

Brauer also said 2020 turnout will be a different animal than a midterm turnout. "This will be Lamb's first election during a presidential year. Special election turnouts are generally low, and midterm election turnouts are usually in the 40% range, though 49% in 2018 was on the higher side than usual, while presidential elections draw in the mid-50s to lower 60s."

A higher turnout with an incumbent president of the opposite party who had previously won the state and the district at the top of the ticket will likely hurt Lamb's chances and bolster Parnell's, said Brauer. "With all that said, Lamb still will have the advantages of incumbency, as well as a district that was made more Democratic with the court-drawn map," he added.

## Pennsylvania 2020: It's Complicated

*November 12, 2019*

Pennsylvania is not a slam-dunk for Donald Trump's reelection campaign.

That's one takeaway from Tuesday's elections, which turned the Philadelphia suburbs even bluer, as Republicans suffered additional congressional losses following last year's midterms. The Democrats have gone from a 13-5 minority in the House to a 9-9 split.

These results in the eastern part of the state "are not helpful to Trump's reelection prospects in Pennsylvania," said Jeff Brauer, political science professor at Keystone College.

"The big question will be the extent of enthusiasm of his nonsupporters in the state," Brauer added. "If that outweighs his base support, that will swing the election against him. It's something he shouldn't underestimate."

Trump won Pennsylvania by just 44,000 votes in 2016, making him the first Republican to take the state since 1988. That margin is so thin that the state could easily be won by a Democrat in 2020.

But if the Democrats want a victory, they must hone their message. Because here's the other takeaway from last week's statewide elections: The western suburbs around Pittsburgh are deepening their allegiance to the GOP.

As Mike Mikus, a Democratic strategist in western Pennsylvania, puts it: "Philadelphia got bluer, and western Pennsylvania got redder." In short, not all suburban voters are alike.

"Go too far left on policy positions like banning fracking or Medicare for All or taking people's guns away anywhere outside of the counties of Philadelphia and they might repeat the same mistakes of 2016," says G. Terry Madonna, political science professor at Franklin and Marshall College.

Plus, voters in Pennsylvania are fickle, which is one reason why it–along with Wisconsin–remains the country's most important swing state. Bucks County, just north of Philadelphia, proves just how easily voters can switch.

In 2016, Bucks County voters favored both Republican Pat Toomey for senator and Democrat Hillary Clinton for president. In 2018, they chose a Republican for Congress, and this year, the county went blue in its municipal elections.

"Voting isn't as cut and dry as outsiders imagine it is," Madonna said. "It can depend on economics, personality, community issues. There are a lot of variables people forget to calculate about what drives a person's vote."

This year, Democrats crushed Republican candidates in suburban Philadelphia's Delaware, Chester and Bucks counties. But Democratic municipal officeholders in the traditionally blue suburban counties around Pittsburgh, such as Beaver, Westmoreland, Washington and Greene, were swept out of county government in favor of Republican candidates. And in commissioners races across the state, Republicans actually flipped more counties than Democrats: Six went from Democrat to Republican, while five went from Republican to Democrat.

Overall, the results were a mixed bag for both parties. But one thing's for sure: Pennsylvania remains the Keystone State to the presidency.

In 2016, Hillary Clinton did what all Democratic presidential nominees have done since 1992: creamed the Republican opponent in Philadelphia and its suburbs. She even flipped then-Republican stronghold Chester County by over 20,000 votes, a spot Barack Obama was unable to win in 2012.

But she essentially lost the rest of the state.

In any other year, this typically isn't a problem. But in 2016, voters in all of the other counties turned out bigly for Trump, handing him the state's total 20 electoral votes.

This deepening Republican support outside of the Philadelphia suburbs remains a threat to the Democratic nominee, a threat that many political professionals ignored in 2016 and continue to ignore to this day.

"The Democrats still have to choose a palatable presidential candidate who has a measured message as an alternative," Brauer said. They must "appeal to working-class Trump voters in order to win the state in 2020."

# America's Troubled Waters

*November 19, 2019*

CRESCO, Iowa–If you come to this rural Iowa town, you'll learn about a problem that may sound familiar.

In The New York Times, for instance, you've learned that many residents in Newark, New Jersey, have gone nearly two years without being able to turn on the faucets in their homes to take a drink of water, cook or even brush their teeth. The culprit: lead-coated pipes that have been seeping their poisons into the homes and schools in a scattering of neighborhoods.

The problem was first ignored and denied. City officials declared the water safe and then took months to admit their error. Eventually, one study revealed that lead had entered the water supply due to corrosion treatment problems at a local plant. Even after the issue was addressed, the federal government found that water filters distributed to residents were ineffective, and the free water they distributed had to be temporarily halted after some bottles had passed their best by date.

"As far as testing reveals, it is only a small portion of the city, but if you are living in that small part of the city, it is a major health risk," explained Seth Siegel, author of "Troubled Water" and the foremost expert on water safety in the country.

The dirty water problem in Flint, Michigan, became a worldwide story.

America's water crisis isn't unique to Newark or Flint, though. People in low-income, majority-minority cities and those in small, rural white communities in Appalachia and the Midwest are suffering every time they turn on the spigot.

The Natural Resources Defense Council studied data compiled through the Safe Drinking Water Act and found that harmful contaminants are found in tap water in every state in the nation.

More than 80,000 violations were reported by community water systems, affecting nearly 77 million people, with 70% of those violations occurring in communities of 500 people or less.

In some cities, water is tainted by decaying lead-laden pipes. In rural areas, it is polluted by contaminants that come from farm fertilizer and pesticides.

"Water safety doesn't pick and choose who it impacts," said Siegel. "It is an issue rural people, city people, suburban people, ex-urban people, Democrats, progressives, Republicans and conservatives are affected by."

"Nobody is immune because it turns out that every city has got contaminants in their water," Siegel said. "It affects the national health profile and the national intelligence. When people are drinking leaded water, it is a confirmed fact that it reduces the IQ of the people who drink that water. And it is confirmed that you are more likely to drop out of high school, that you're more likely to get involved with crime if you have been drinking leaded water."

Rural areas are particularly at risk. They tend to be serviced by small, underfunded utilities, or they are using private drinking wells that are not regulated by the Environmental Protection Agency.

In the 1,100 miles that separate Newark from Cresco, hundreds of smaller towns in Appalachia and the Midwest face the same perilous crisis as the larger cities. But their issues remain largely unknown. Out here, the news coverage is scant, sometimes because no local paper exists.

Yet fertilizers and coal mine leakage often find their way into wells and rural water systems that could harm the residents.

Hunter Slifka is part of changing that problem. The 23-year-old wanted to make a difference in his hometown of Cresco.

He found his path after getting a degree in conservation management at Upper Iowa University and coming back to work for the Howard County Soil and Water Conservation District.

He's also the local high school's wrestling coach. Now he's focused on removing nitrates and bacteria in the area's streams and groundwater.

These soil and water conservation districts across the American agriculture heartland, funded by the Department of Agriculture as well as local downriver utilities, are putting in natural barriers that reduce or eliminate the amount of fertilizer and pesticides that get into groundwater and runoff into rivers.

"Water is the great connector in communities, and the quality of it affects everyone," Slifka told me. "My goal was to make sure we were able to have safe water for people who live on the farms here but also enough water for farmers to have for their crops."

Siegel says the solution for everyone will come "when people understand that their children's health, IQ and futures are at risk, when their own fertility is at risk and when they realize that cancers come from many of these chemicals. When people understand all this, they will demand action."

Siegel says when there is a popular will for change, there will be transformation.

"Whether they're in rural America or urban America, where they're fancy, elite people, whether they're simple, dirt-under-the-fingernails people, it's going to be the same," he said. "That's when politicians find the nerve to act."

## Dr. Laura's Lasting Truths

*November 26, 2019*

When Dr. Laura Schlessinger got her foot entangled with shards of broken glass a few months ago, she cleaned the wound, cringed at the amount of blood and went about her business despite a lingering, stinging pain that nagged at her to do something.

Apropos of what she does in her professional life as the host of the "Dr. Laura" program on satellite radio, she yielded to the warning signs and went to the doctor, who informed her there were several pieces still lodged in her foot.

She had them removed and then kept them as a reminder of sorts to listen to those uncomfortable things we need to address in our lives, and in fact, to look them square in the eye every once in a while so you don't make that same mistake twice.

At 72, Schlessinger is many things.

Her 40-year radio career in which she dispenses blunt, pragmatic advice that sometimes pushes, sometimes guides and sometimes delivers a kick in the gut recently earned her an induction to the National Radio Hall of Fame.

She is also a mom, an exhaustive Lego builder, a sailor, a pool shark, a tennis player, a jeweler and a powerlifter who adores her daughter-in-law and loves to hike, go shooting, ride her Harley and wear as much pink as possible in every way she can.

Schlessinger described her tattoo. "On my left shoulder is a beautiful rendition of a skull–not the kind of stuff you see on Hells

Angels. It's got a rose in its mouth," she explained. "I said to the guy; I'm really kind of a bad-ass girly girl. People kind of keep trying to pin me down. You're this conservative, tight-ass broad. No. I'm not. I'm quite complex. I'll stand by a door all day until the guy opens it. I can kick the door down because I'm a black belt, but I wait for a guy to open it, and I thank him very cordially."

Listen to her Sirius XM show with any regularity and you notice the relationship she has with her listeners is deep, complex, loyal, loving and connected. Oftentimes after she delivers a harsh assessment of a listener's problem, he or she will concede, "I knew you were going to tell me that."

Industry insiders say that not only has her popularity not ceded any ground but it has grown, in particular among young conservative women and men.

Her newest book, "Love and Life" (she has 12 New York Times bestsellers under her belt), is a collection of her columns over the past 15 years that cover a broad spectrum of the complexities of life and love. It's a book of the truths that have stood the test of time in the way a good movie holds up long after the scenery in the world has changed. This is nothing short of astounding, given our rapidly changing culture.

"Frankly, nothing changes," she said. "The human heart, the needs of children, the pains of disappointment, frustration, and loss, the expectations not met. The fear of taking on challenges–I mean that and more. That's a constant throughout all humanity from day one in the Bible for goodness sake."

She added: "And that's why all this holds up because there are some basic truths that regardless of the era and the new popular thought–the truth is there are things women need, there are things men need, there are things children need, there are things parents need, there are things friends need. It doesn't change. It never has."

She is correct. Humans need words and contact to feel safe. People need to *give* as a way of feeling good. In short, people need to have a purpose in their lives in order to build a life more meaningful than just accumulating goodies. Our culture today doesn't agree.

"Our culture is horrible," she said. "Look at the meanness. And it comes from our media and the internet in particular because anonymity allows people to have their dark side implemented without any restraint. Human beings need restraint. That's why we have religion, we have rules, we have morality because we're quite aware that we as human beings can run the gamut from compassion domiciled."

One of her favorite parts of the book is the afterword, whose subtitle, "96 Kinds of People Who Hate Dr. Laura (and Dr. Laura Loves It!)," reveals her quirky sense of humor. Schlessinger's haters attempted to cancel her long before "canceling" became a vindictive verb. She says they are hilarious. And she's not wrong.

# In the 'Nicest Place in America,' Community Thrives

*December 3, 2019*

COLUMBIANA, Ohio–The thing about a city earning a title such as the "nicest place in America" is that outsiders often assume the people who live there don't have to work at being nice.

Well, anyone in this lovely city that straddles both the Mahoning and Columbiana Counties would say you do have to work at it. But like anything worthwhile in this world (including warmth, generosity, common courtesy and the selfless notion of paying it forward), it starts to come more easily with time.

It also helps that Columbiana has a deep sense of community, which means it is deeply committed to its success. People here are involved in the church, civic groups and the general betterment of the city.

It's not because it is a small city or because it oozes the type of charm Hallmark aims to capture in its Christmas movies. It's because everyone in town has a hand, large or small, in the community's health and well-being.

Spend less than five minutes with City Manager Lance Willard and you'll know exactly what I mean. Just before the annual Christmas parade, ask for his rundown on why his city earned the status of "nicest place" from Reader's Digest, and you'll get a pretty vivid picture.

Spend an additional five minutes with Willard and you'll find out why this city of 6,200 is prospering economically, growing in population and expanding its charming Main Street with innovative retail opportunities such as pop-ups and shared retail spaces. Its success has attracted the attention of nearby Rust Belt towns looking to replicate.

"I've had other communities call us–Salem, Lisbon, East Liverpool, Leetonia, Warren, Zanesville–and they're saying, 'Hey, what are you guys doing up there?'" Willard said of the string of neighboring cities and towns looking for guidance on economic development including how to procure grants for new infrastructure and attract small businesses.

His answer? "I just send them a zip file of what we've been doing."

None of Columbiana's success has come at the expense of the soul of the city–it has only made it nicer.

"If I could point to one place that embodies who the people of Columbiana are, I would point to Crown Productions at the Main Street Theater, where they showcase theater productions that feature only actors with special needs," Willard said just before those actors were set to load up on the first float to drive down Main Street in the annual parade.

All around the charming grid and city square is evidence of the things needed to keep a community together: plenty of churches and faith-based community groups holding their own, a phenomenon that many sister Rust Belt towns and cities have lost.

And with that loss comes decay, addiction, broken families and flight.

"All of our traditional organizations are very much intact," said Willard.

The Crown Theater special needs group was critical to the community's winning the Reader's Digest contest, explained Willard: "Mary Lou Wilson wrote a story to them explaining about her grandson who has disabilities and is in his 40s who finally flowered, if you will, in the local theater program. Without her story, which you need at least a box of Kleenex beside you to read, the designation would have never happened."

Willard wasn't elected to be city manager; he was voted on by members of the city council. While the mayor presides over the council and is involved in the community, the city manager runs day-to-day operations, sort of like a CEO.

The six council members are all elected on an at-large basis, with no party allowed to hold more than three seats.

For the most part, Willard explains, the council doesn't put a team jersey on when it comes to the city: "It is not partisan politics. It is actual effective governing."

It helps that everyone on the council is pretty even-keeled. That's not surprising, though, in the "nicest place in America."

This story isn't about small towns or small cities being better than large cities or large metropolitan areas. It is about a city that understands the value of community and everyone taking the time to invest in it. It's not uniquely Columbiana; it's uniquely American. Yet sometimes we lose our way in trying to be the best or the first in things that don't help the community and only help our feelings in the moment.

There is a little Columbiana in all of us. We should work on remembering that every day.

# He Makes a Village

*December 10, 2019*

SAVANNAH, Georgia–Tyler Merritt has taken the saying "It takes a village to raise a child" and turned it a bit sideways. He's building a village, literally, to allow adults to raise themselves up. His village is a stabilizing rail, or a steppingstone to a better life.

Merritt, a former Army captain and special operations air mission commander, is trying to help his military brothers and sisters who have found themselves post-military service and one paycheck away from financial collapse, as well as those struggling to find their way through modern civilian life, which does not begin and end with a stated purpose in the way military service does.

"Our most recent initiative is our veterans village," said Merritt, whose post-military life makes him an unlikely entrepreneur and philanthropist as the CEO of Nine Line Apparel and president of Nine Line Foundation.

Merritt is standing outside the massive apparel store he founded in 2012 that quickly went from a handful of employees, mostly family, to a staff of more than 240, mostly veterans. He's also built up a deeply loyal cross-country customer base for the company's patriotic gear.

He is unassuming and charming, and he never sits still. On this bright and warm Georgia day, Merritt is pacing back and forth, phone in hand, trying to connect airline executives with families who lost loved ones in a military training accident and get them to their family members as quickly as possible.

The Nine Line facility has a retail component that does brisk business despite being located far from the downtown Savannah business district. Inside, employees are making the shirts and gear for the online and storefront retail operations. Outside, a model of one of the tiny houses Merritt is building for homeless veterans sits proudly for anyone to tour.

He's built 20 of them. Well, he and 100 of his closest friends (of which he has an eclectic assortment). All he did was put one Facebook post up saying he needed help building 20 tiny homes for veterans, and people from all walks of life responded accordingly, with a community forming around his dream of providing temporary housing for homeless veterans.

That community became the village.

"We had food brought in, and we had some entertainment and some interesting characters," he said modestly as he peeled off names of WWE wrestlers who are big fans of Nine Line. "The Undertaker was down here. We had Dustin Rhodes, Diamond Dallas Page, some country music stars, too: Craig Morgan and Luke Combs."

He added: "The red-blooded Americans that not only follow them but also follow us just showed up, along with skilled laborers and people in the community to help bang nails together. Those who are not skilled laborers–they bring the camaraderie."

Statistics from the Department of Veterans Affairs show that homeless veterans are predominantly male and make up approximately 11% of all adult homelessness. Almost half served during the Vietnam era.

Merritt described his interaction with the Chatham Savannah Authority for the Homeless. "When we first met with the homeless authority, they asked what we can do, and I said, basically, 'let's get started now.'"

Nine Line has also partnered with Georgia Southern University, which will provide vocational training and career counseling along with a new aquaponics center it is building right here on the sprawling apparel-making property.

"We're going to have a beautiful 80-foot-by-40-foot, state-of-the-art aquaponics center that's going to be the training initiative for these homeless veterans," he explained. "They're going to be transported here and taught a skill set of how to manage this highly complex agricultural environment where fish feed plants, plants feed fish."

The produce that is harvested will go toward physically healing them, but the excess produce will also be sold at places such as farmers markets, with all the money going back into the foundation initiatives.

"So, it's an idea of this venture entrepreneurism that it truly become a representation of what we're trying to accomplish, which is a self-contained ecosystem," he said.

Merritt said the initiative holds no galas to snag big donors. Nor does it get government assistance. This is all by design. "That's not us," he says. "We do barbecues. We do shooting matches. We have things that are completely donated, and all the proceeds go towards these initiatives and, eventually, this aquaponics center. It's all with a purpose, and it is all self-sustaining. That's how you build communities and villages."

# A Different Kind of Celebrity on Twitter

*December 17, 2019*

RUSSELLTON, Pennsylvania–Despite his natural shyness, Trevor Donovan has shined in an occupation that demands extroversion both on the job and off. The Hollywood actor, who is currently best known for his roles in the highly popular Hallmark Channel Christmas movies, overcame his social awkwardness by deciding to utilize his high profile for a greater purpose.

This resolution ultimately brought the former "90210" star here to Deer Lakes Middle School, located in a suburban Pittsburgh school district, where he discussed his own experiences with being bullied and reminded children that their words have impact–especially on social media.

In an era when entertainers, politicians, sports figures and academics often use social media as a sledgehammer against those with "bad" opinions or allegiances, frequently destroying or "canceling" themselves or their victims, Donovan's Twitter feed is part beacon of hope.

"We have very few adults who offer young people examples of how to behave on social media," middle school counselor Jackie Jaros said. "Donovan has a unique skill and story to tell the students about how to use social media positively."

"He leads by example," said Jaros, who kicked off the assembly with a handful of students lined up at a table on the stage, all competing to see who could empty a full tube of toothpaste onto a paper plate first.

When the toothpaste contest was thrown in reverse to see who could put the toothpaste back in the tube the fastest, the lesson unfolded: Despite their best efforts to get it back in the tube, there was more paste on the paper plate than in any of the tubes.

"The lesson was clear: The same thing happens with our words," Jaros explained. "When you say something to somebody, you may go to try to take it back with an apology or with your actions, but it's out there."

"Once the words are said, they never go away," she said.

Located on a former coal patch, the region surrounding the school district is a mix of tidy middle-class homes, a spattering of centuries-old log houses and affluence. The area has farms, industry, a mansion or two, and plenty of deer scurrying along the winding roads that lead to the banks of the Allegheny River.

Donovan's plan in his youth was to be a graphic artist. His younger brother became a fireman. "I grew up in a little house that's built in 1915, 20 minutes south of Mammoth, base of a mountain," he recalled of a childhood he describes as ideal and unpretentious. "It was a gas station until the mid-'70s. And it was converted, so it's over a hundred years old now. And I used to wake up stacked with comforters and stuff, plenty warm, but I'd wake up in the morning; there'd be snow on the foot of my bed because of the crack in the wall that a blizzard would come through."

Hallmark movies, of which Donovan has done nine, have made the Hallmark Channel a powerhouse. Last holiday season alone, the channel attracted almost 70 million unique viewers.

Those successes don't just happen because of the channel's name brand. It is the people in the movies, such as Donovan, who are viewed as integral to the Hallmark experience. Many viewers consider the character and the actors part of their family, according to Hallmark CEO Bill Abbott.

"Trevor is just the person with the biggest heart," Abbott said, "somebody who deeply cares about issues and people and animals, too. He is just a breath of fresh air, a man who is genuine, who is thoughtful, in an era where there are far too many people and much less talented actors in the world who don't always do things for the right reasons."

Abbot adds that Donovan's social media presence is a reflection of everything he tries to cultivate for the Hallmark brand. Donovan is relieved because he says he's just being himself.

"I like showing my fitness routines, my love for dogs, my love for visiting Pittsburgh," he says jokingly before turning back to his passion for helping young people. "I want to be a positive influence on the social media platform. And it's a slower burn, I think, to become more recognized. ... It's easy to make a big negative comment that gets a bunch of people angry, and all of a sudden you're viral or famous. But I wouldn't feel right because it's not me. And besides, that comes at a cost; it's not true to who I am nor true to a greater purpose of wanting to be a stable influence on our young people."

# The Town That Wouldn't Be Passed by

*December 24, 2019*

EVERETT, Pennsylvania–For the past two years, items on layaway for over 200 families at the Walmart here have been paid for by some generous soul who won't reveal his or her identity. Last year, this modern St. Nicholas paid off $46,000 in items placed on layaway by local residents. This year's total was $40,000.

Nestled in the narrows between the Raystown Branch of the Juniata River and the Tussey Mountain ridge of the Appalachian Mountains, Everett was originally called Bloody Run.

Like many frontier towns with peculiar names derived from dubious tales, the townspeople, through a vote, changed the name to Everett to honor Edward Everett, the famed orator and former Massachusetts governor. History students will know Everett as the man who gave the rather long-winded speech ahead of Abraham Lincoln's Gettysburg Address.

The town of Everett prospered over the years. Not too big, not too small, its location was everything from the dawn of the stagecoach to the jalopy. It's the midway point on the journey from Philadelphia to Pittsburgh.

The town toyed with Industrial Revolution fame in 1899 when Chester Karns, the son of the local carriage-maker, built an automobile by hand–and then built another and another and another.

Known as the Karns Runabout, Karns understood he needed capital for a factory to produce his automobile. As local legend goes, he petitioned the government for a loan around the same time a man from Detroit named Henry Ford did, and we all know the rest of that story.

A lot of folks who look at Everett on a map might be tempted to quip that this town has been passed by one too many times to be relevant in today's world of ascending technologies that dominate every aspect of our lives.

A lot of folks would be wrong. There is an incredible heart to Everett that captivates you the moment you turn left off of the bypass road that's supposed to help you skip the Lincoln Highway, where the center of the town hums.

You'll get to Bedford, Pittsburgh or Ohio faster if you take the bypass, but then you'd miss Pinky's hair salon, delightful Christmas decorations on Main Street, The Igloo ice cream shop that is literally shaped as a chocolate-covered igloo or the Bloody Run mural celebrating Everett's storied history.

Any other town would have died–many have–when a bypass was created to avoid the 25 mph speed zones (15 mph during school hours). But Everett didn't. It has stayed vibrant as well as generous in the 50 years since the federal highway system all but erased it from the traveling landscape.

And if you bypass the town, you will likely miss the very reason the anonymous donor decided to help families with their Christmas layaways. If you see the town, you see that folks here pay it forward every day of the year just as many Americans do, without fanfare and without attention for their good deeds.

Need a coat during the brisk months in the narrows? No worries; just go to the library, where anyone who needs a warm winter coat can feel free to take their pick from a variety of very nice coats and jackets just inside the library doors.

In December, Santa just happens to be volunteering there. You can get your photo taken with him in his sleigh.

The town also sponsors a home-decorating contest, a parking meter-decorating contest and a business-decorating contest. The festivities here are serious.

That is because it seems everyone here clings to the sense of community that keeps its citizenry connected, stable and engaged.

They understand, as do millions of other Americans, that the most important things have not passed their town by, even in the toughest of times. Faith, compassion and community have persisted.

It is likely that whoever donated the money for the layaways here in Everett grew up in the warm embrace of the town's grace and character. It is also likely that this character is what inspired him or her to give back.

Here's what might surprise you the most: I think America is mostly this way. At least, America is more like Everett than it is like whatever you see on cable news. You just sometimes have to slow down to see it.

# The Great Revolt Enters a New Phase: How the Populist Uprising of 2016 Will Reverberate in 2020

*December 31, 2019*

WESTBY, WISCONSIN–In a country increasingly engaged in national politics and divided, the next 12 months may feel like 12 years. Voters in both trenches are eager to vote, convinced not only of victory but also of vindication. The shocking result in 2016 wasn't a black swan, an irregular election deviating from normalcy, but instead the indicator of the realignment we describe in "The Great Revolt: Inside the Populist Coalition Reshaping American Politics," now available in a new a paperback edition in time for the 2020 election season.

The story of America's evolving political topography is one of tectonic plates that slowly grind against one another until a break notably alters the landscape with seismic consequences–a sudden lurch long in development. The election of President Donald Trump cemented a realignment of the two political parties rooted in cultural and economic change years in the making. Although he has been the epicenter of all politics since his announcement of candidacy in 2015, Trump is the product of this realignment more than its cause, a fact that becomes clear as you travel the back roads to the places that made him the most unlikely president of our era.

Thirty-year-old dairy farmer Ben Klinkner doesn't consider himself a member of either political part. "I am a Christian conservative," he says matter-of-factly.

Sitting at conference table at the Westby Co-op Credit Union, the sixth-generation family farmer who has a master's degree in meat science explains that when he left to attend college at the University of Wisconsin-River Falls, and then at North Dakota State University in Fargo for his master's, he vowed he would never milk a cow again.

"And I've been doing just that every day for the past six years," he said.

On Trump, Klinkner is pragmatic. "I am very happy with his policies. I just wish he'd put that Twitter down," he said of the president's unorthodox style of communicating. This cuts against the national media's narrative that farmers will dump the president because of the trade uncertainty.

And, yes, Klinkner will vote for him again.

Trump's 2016 victory came in spite of his historically weak performance in the suburbs long dominated by Republicans. The key was that he more than overcame his suburban weakness with the mass conversion of blue-collar voters in ancestrally Democratic bastions of the Midwest, and he inspired irregular voters who mistrust both parties. For "The Great Revolt," we traveled to the counties in the Great Lakes states that Trump wrested away from Democratic heritage to find examples of the voter archetypes that define the Trump coalition.

Large strata of the population are now not just eager to vote in the next race for president but eager to vote against the party of their ancestry. This enthusiasm for new alliances is perhaps the greatest indicator of lasting realignment.

The election of Trump glued populism to conservatism, an ideology long leavened by anti-establishment rhetoric but rooted in the inertial acquiescence to the status quo that comes with laissez-faire policies. In Trump, Republicans have embraced, or have been forced to embrace, a more muscular and activist approach on issues ranging from trade policy to nonstop legal warfare with liberal state governments like California's. Gone is the consistency of federalism, replaced in conservatism's pantheon with the base-motivating potency of perpetual confrontation.

The emotional exertion of Trump's combative approach continues to provide Democrats with avenues of appeal to buttoned-up suburbanites who otherwise resist liberal policies. And it has forced populists on the left to copy Trump's antagonistic style, elevating Sens. Elizabeth Warren and Bernie Sanders, the edgiest of the Democratic contenders for president, into front-runners.

Democratic populists seek to copy Trump's success but not to win back the same populist voters who flipped margins by 32 points from 2012 to 2016 in places like Ashtabula, Ohio, or 18 points in Erie, Pennsylvania, both of which we profiled in "The Great Revolt." Democrats such as Warren and Sanders have given up on winning those places–and those Obama voters.

Instead, Sanders and Warren hope to emulate Trump's success with their party's version of the voters we called Perotistas, those whose participation in elections is irregular, even elliptical, and who pass into voting booths every decade or so like comets crashing into an otherwise orderly solar system, only to disappear just as abruptly.

For his part, the president has accepted his path, choosing not to broaden his appeal by tapering his temperament to one that might suit the two-income, two-degree Republican-leaning suburban families who split their tickets in 2016 and then chose Democratic congressmen in 2018. These voters crave predictability and civility at a gut level, two things in short supply in Trump's style, but they tell pollsters they are wary of the lurch toward socialism in today's Democratic Party. Thus far, their hearts have overpowered their heads in off-year elections in the Trump era, and Democrats are banking on the same result in 2020.

Whether or not the president ever turns his attention to winning over the voters who resist both socialism and his own style, other Republicans will be appealing to them. Suburban voters hold the keys to hotly contested 2020 Senate races in Michigan, North Carolina, Arizona and Colorado–not to mention the entire slate of competitive House districts.

The suburbs may be where control of government will be decided, but the 2020 election will not be the end of the coalition Trump mobilized in 2016 or the resistance that formed in response. Why? Because the individualization of our cultural economy and the self-sorting of our communities will keep fueling distrust of establishment institutions and keep roiling our political and consumer behaviors. Establishment politicians, CEOs and journalists all ignore the dynamism of this great revolt at their own peril.

# About the Author

Salena Zito has held a long, successful career as a national political reporter. Born and bred in Pittsburgh, she worked for the Pittsburgh Tribute-Review for 11 years. She has interviewed every U.S. president and vice president since 1992, as well as top leaders in Washington, D.C., including secretaries of state, speakers of the House and U.S. Central Command generals. Her passion, though, is interviewing thousands of people across the country. She reaches the Everyman and Everywoman through the lost art of shoe-leather journalism, having traveled along the back roads of 49 states.

Salena joined the New York Post in September 2016. She acts as a CNN political analyst, and a staff reporter and columnist for the Washington Examiner.

She rarely misses Sunday dinner with her overly loud Italian Scots-Irish family. She is the mother of two adult children, a grandmother, an avid cyclist and hiker, a baseball fan and a U.S. history geek.

*IT'S COMPLICATED*
is also available as an e-book
for Kindle, Amazon Fire, iPad, Nook and
Android e-readers. Visit
creatorspublishing.com to learn more.

o o o

### CREATORS PUBLISHING

We publish books.
We find compelling storytellers and
help them craft their narrative,
distributing their novels and collections
worldwide.

o o o

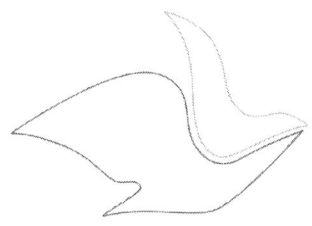

Made in the USA
Middletown, DE
24 August 2023

37319764R00106